ALL SONDHEIM

VOL. IV MUSIC AND LYRICS BY STEPHEN SONDHEIM

Contents

Vocal Selections Prepared by: Paul McKibbins
Project Manager: Sy Feldman
Cover Photography: Michael Le Poer Trench

© 1999 ALFRED PUBLISHING
All Rights Reserved

Any duplication, adaptation or arrangement of the compositions
contained in this collection requires the written consent of the Publisher.
No part of this book may be photocopied or reproduced in any way without permission.

Academy Award ® Winner
From the Motion Picture "Dick Tracy

Sooner Or Later
(I Always Get My Man)

Music and Lyrics by
Stephen Sondheim

© 1990 RILTING MUSIC, INC. and TOUCHSTONE PICTURES MUSIC & SONGS, INC.
All Rights on behalf of RILTING MUSIC, INC. Administered by WB MUSIC CORP.
All Rights Reserved

Ba - by, it's time that you faced it. I al - ways get my
mp
dim.
man.
p
mp
p
mp
Soon - er or lat - er you're gon - na de - cide:
p
mp
Soon - er or lat - er there's no - where to hide.
p

Ba - by, it's time, so why waste it in chat - ter? Let's
mp
cresc.
set - tle the mat - ter.
dim.
poco cresc.
Ba - by, you're mine on a plat - ter, I al - ways get my
dim.
p
man. But
p
mp

if you in - sist, babe, the chal- lenge de - lights me. The more you re - sist, babe, the
more it ex - cites me. And no one I've kissed, babe,
ev - er fights me a - gain. If
legato, poco cresc.
dim.
you're on my list, it's just a ques - tion of
mf
mp

when.
When I ___ get a yen,
legato
mf
p
non legato
Then ba - by, a - men.
I'm count - ing to
cresc. poco a poco
ten, ___
And
then ___
molto rall.

Tempo Primo - Molto Maestoso
I'm gon-na love you like no-thing you've known.
I'm gon-na love you, and you all a - lone.
Soon-er is bet-ter than lat-er but lov-er, I'll
hov-er, I'll plan.

1.
A tempo
This time I'm not on - ly get-ting, I'm hold - ing my man.
mf
poco rall.
mp
2.
This time I'm not on - ly get- ting, I'm hold - ing my
mf
man.
poco rall.

From the Film Musical "Singing Out Loud"

Dawn

Music and Lyrics by
Stephen Sondheim

© 1992, 1993 RILTING MUSIC, INC.
All Rights Administered by WB MUSIC CORP.
International Copyright Secured All Rights Reserved

ten.
caught half - way__ be-tween yes - ter - day__ And to - mor - row.
ten.
Animato, ma non troppo (♩ = 176)
mf
DAISY:
ten.
Walk - ing home From work - ing late,__ And a - round the bend— Dawn . . .__
ten.
sub.
f
sfz
__ You may look grim__ But you feel just great,__'Cause you've got this friend:
sub. mp

poco rall.
ten.
Dawn. You're both half-way be-tween yes - ter - day And to -
sub. f sfz mf
poco rall.
a tempo
mor-row.
mp
a tempo
Not a street that does-n't have a shine, Not a sound ex-cept the
mf
milk-man's rat - tle, Not a stream of sev-en mil - lion cat - tle, And the

cit - y's mine
Yours and mine,
Dawn!
cresc.
sub. mp
mf
It's when the
Rubato
moon's gone down, But the sun's not up, Just be - fore this
sub. mp
molto legato
poco rall.
great big town Be - comes a great big but - ter - cup. Your
poco rall.

a tempo
feet are sore, You're feel - ing weird, And then there it comes
a tempo
mf sempre leggiero
ten.
Dawn.
The
ten.
sub. f
sfz
cit - y's roar May have dis - ap - peared, But the cit - y hums...
mf
Dawn!
sub. f

Not a street that is - n't clean and still,
MILKMAN:
Not a wall that does - n't
Dawn!
gleam and glis - ten,
STREETCLEANER:
Not a roof that is - n't gold And lis - ten, not a
Dawn!
sin - gle drill
What a thrill!
Dawn!
MEN:
What a thrill!
Dawn!

Dawn!
Dawn!
MILKMAN:
And so you're
Poco rubato
on your own, And you do feel fright-ened, On - ly
STREETCLEANER:
On - ly though you're

DAISY:
OTHERS:
When it's
all a - lone,___ Some-how you simp - ly don't feel lone - ly When it's
a tempo
dawn!___
half past four, You're half a - wake___ And the town is dead
a tempo
ALL:
Yawn!___
You

think, what more can a per - son take, And then o - ver - head:
mf
Dawn!
Calm and qui - et though the cit - y seems,
Dead a - sleep it's still a -
live and teem - ing,
What with sev - en mil - lion peo - ple dream - ing Sev - en

mil - lion dreams Of course it gleams! You watch the
Poco rubato
stars go one by one, You see the first sign
of the sun. It makes you feel that done is done And
cresc.
bet - ter things Have just be - gun It's called

a tempo
Dawn!
a tempo

From the Film "The Thing Of It Is"

No, Mary Ann

Music and Lyrics by
Stephen Sondheim

Con brio

© 1969 (Unpublished) Stephen Sondheim
© 1999 RILTING MUSIC, INC.
All Rights Administererd by WB MUSIC CORP.
All Rights Reserved

Sym-pho-ny orch - es-tras reel - ing In glo - ri - ous song,
Noth-ing but beau - ti - ful feel - ing, Boy, were you wrong!
Now you say life is a bore. No, Mar - y Ann.
mf
sim.
Drear-y and gray and no more. No, Mar - y Ann.

Say it's all pink,
Say it's all gray,
That's too ea - sy to think
And too ea - sy to say.
And I'm just a man,
Mar - y Ann.
f
3
fz
mp
come sopra
p

You thought it all would be pie.
No, Ma - ry Ann.
mf
Pink lit - tle birds in the sky.
No, Ma - ry Ann.
Sym-pho - ny or - ches-tras
reel - ing In glo - ri - ous song,

Noth-ing but beau - ti - ful feel - ing, Boy, were you wrong!
Sud-den-ly now it's all flat. No, Mar-y Ann.
f
Drear-y and gray and that's that. No, Mar - y Ann.
Say it's all pink, Say it's all gray, That's too
cresc. poco a poco

ea - sy to think And too ea - sy to say. It's what you feel And
ff
that's the least of it. Make a meal No, make a feast of it! The
thing of it is: I love you, Mar - y Ann!

From the Film Musical "Singing Out Loud"

Sand

Music and Lyrics by
Stephen Sondheim

© 1992, 1993 by RILTING MUSIC, INC.
All Rights Administered by WB MUSIC CORP.
International Copyright Secured All Rights Reserved Used by Permission

Love is just sand, slip-ping through your fing - ers. Now it's in hand, now it is - n't there.
Just like sand, e - ven when it ling - ers, All it's a - bout is, you
can't get it out of your hair.
It can seem smooth when real-ly it's bump - y, It can look soft and be dry,

Warm and be sooth - ing, hot and make you jump - y, Al - though you'll nev - er know un - til you
try:
Is it the Sa - ha - ra or a beach be - neath the Car - ib - be - an
rit.
rit.
sky? . . .
a tempo
Love is just sand,
a tempo
you can feel it shift - ing. Soon as you stand, you be - gin to sink.

Ev - 'ry - thing's planned, Then it gets to drift - ing, Nev - er to where you think

rit. poco a poco
Love ain't sol - id land, It's just sand . . .
rit. poco a poco

rit.
Noth-ing but sand . . .
mp
legato
rit.

Cut from the Musical "Follies"

The World's Full Of Girls

Music and Lyrics by
Stephen Sondheim

© 1971 RANGE ROAD MUSIC, INC., QUARTET MUSIC, INC., RILTING MUSIC, INC. and BURTHEN MUSIC CO., INC.
All Rights Administered by CARLIN AMERICA, INC.
All Rights Reserved Used by Permission

Wait - ing to be kissed,
Oops! There's one I missed! The
world's full of girls And I'm mak - ing up a list 'Cause I'm
gon - na kiss 'em Each and ev - 'ry one. And
when, And when I've

kissed 'em all And sat - is - fied my yen, What
then? What then? I
guess I'm gon - na have to kiss 'em o - ver a - gain. The
world's full of girls Who are vir - gin - al and pink,
f

Young - er than you think,
How a - bout a drink? The
world's full of girls And be - fore I start to sink, I am
gon - na kiss 'em, Each and ev - 'ry one!

GIRL I:
BEN:
You miss Me? Yes, you with the Mar - i - lyn Mon -

GIRL I:
BEN:
GIRL I:
roe . . . Who? . . . Hair - do . . . Who the fuck is Mar - i - lyn Mon -
BEN:
roe? Yes, well then, You, shall we blow the joint And
GIRL II:
BEN:
go out twist - ing? Go out what? I see your point. Well,
you then Pret - ty maid - en, Shall we

GIRL III:
sit and have a chat? I could go for that.
BEN:
Good, then. Pret - ty maid - en, Shall we
GIRL III:
BEN: GIRL III:
has - ten to my flat. What a pus - sy - cat! Now . . . I
cer - tain - ly am hon - ored that a gen - tle - man like you wants to

take a girl like me Out for a date When you could prob - ab - ly Have
an - y - one at all Like a star Or a duch - ess, Say do
you know Prin - cess Grace? I mean, well what's she real - ly like? 'Cause I
gath - er from your book, Al - though I did - n't real - ly read it, That you

know a lot of big And im - por - tant cel - eb - ri - ties That
pic - ture on the jack - et Does - n't real - ly do you jus - tice, You're more
hand - some in the flesh With all that gray - ing in your hair, But then I've
al - ways gone for old - er men Which should - n't hang you up But an

aw - ful lot of old - er men Get ter - ri - bly up - tight Like out in
pub - lic When we bump in - to friends, But if an - y - thing, it's
me Who feels em - bar - rassed But I'm not, 'Cause like I said, How I'm
hon - ored And so what if peo - ple think I'm be - ing kept or some-thing?

mf
PHYLLIS:
The
world's full of boys Who are wait - ing to be kissed,
Wait - ing to be kissed, Well, if you in - sist . . . The

world's full of boys, And I hard - ly can re - sist, So I'm
gon - na kiss 'em each and ev - 'ry one. And
when, And when I've
BOYS:
kissed 'em all And sat - is - fied my yen. What

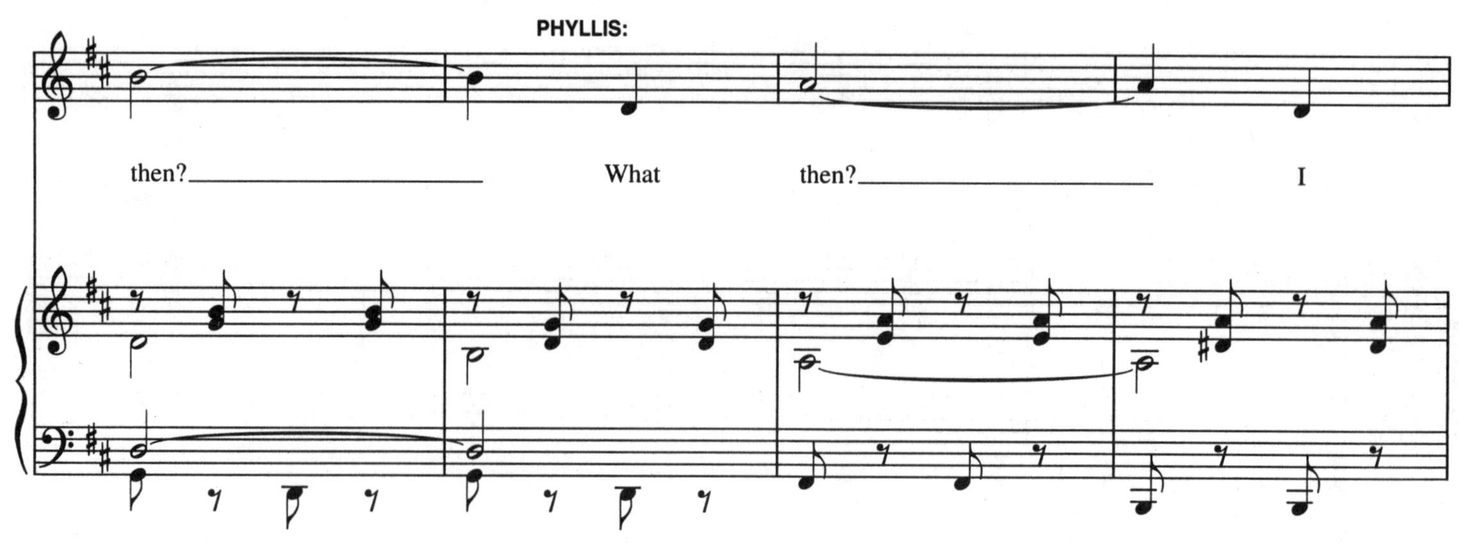
PHYLLIS:
then?
What
then?
I

guess I'm gon - na have to kiss 'em o - ver a - gain.
The
sub. p

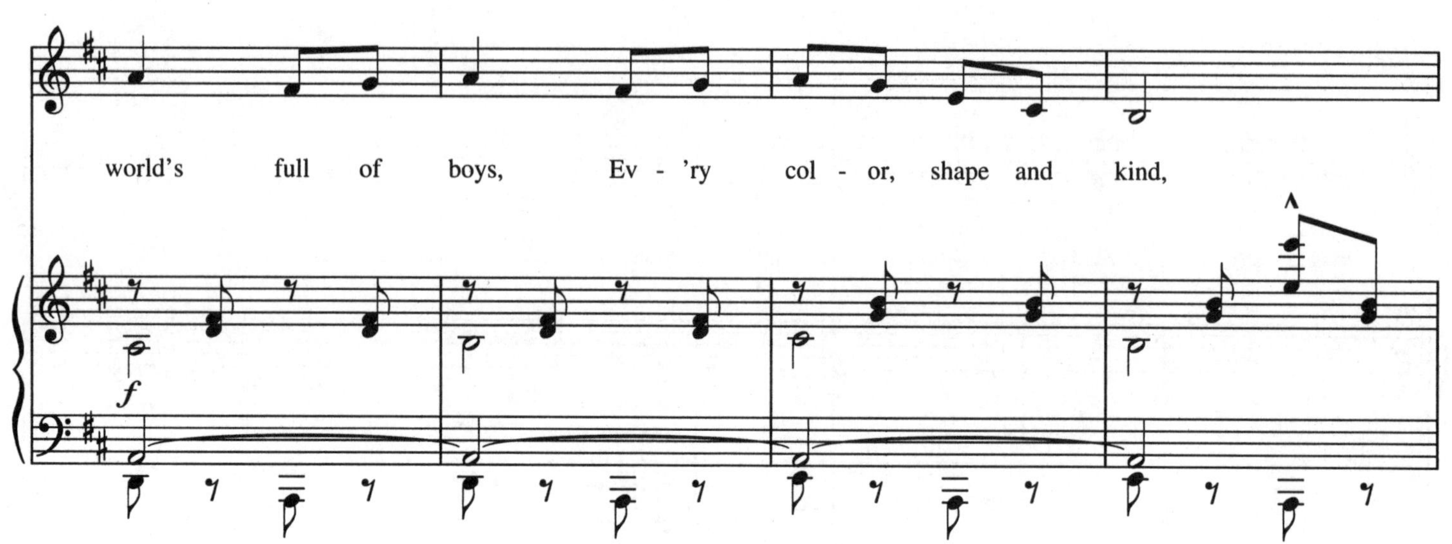
world's full of boys, Ev - 'ry col - or, shape and kind,
f

Raun - chy and re - fined. Look at that be - hind. The

world's full of boys, And I'm sure you would - n't mind If I

go and sleep with each and ev - 'ry one.

From the unproduced TV Musical "Do You Hear A Waltz?"

Do I Hear A Waltz?

Music and Lyrics by
Stephen Sondheim

Moderato (♩. = 60)

© 1998 by RILTING MUSIC, INC.
All Rights Administered by WB MUSIC CORP.
International Copyright Secured All Rights Reserved Used by Permission

where is the band?
A rose is a rose,

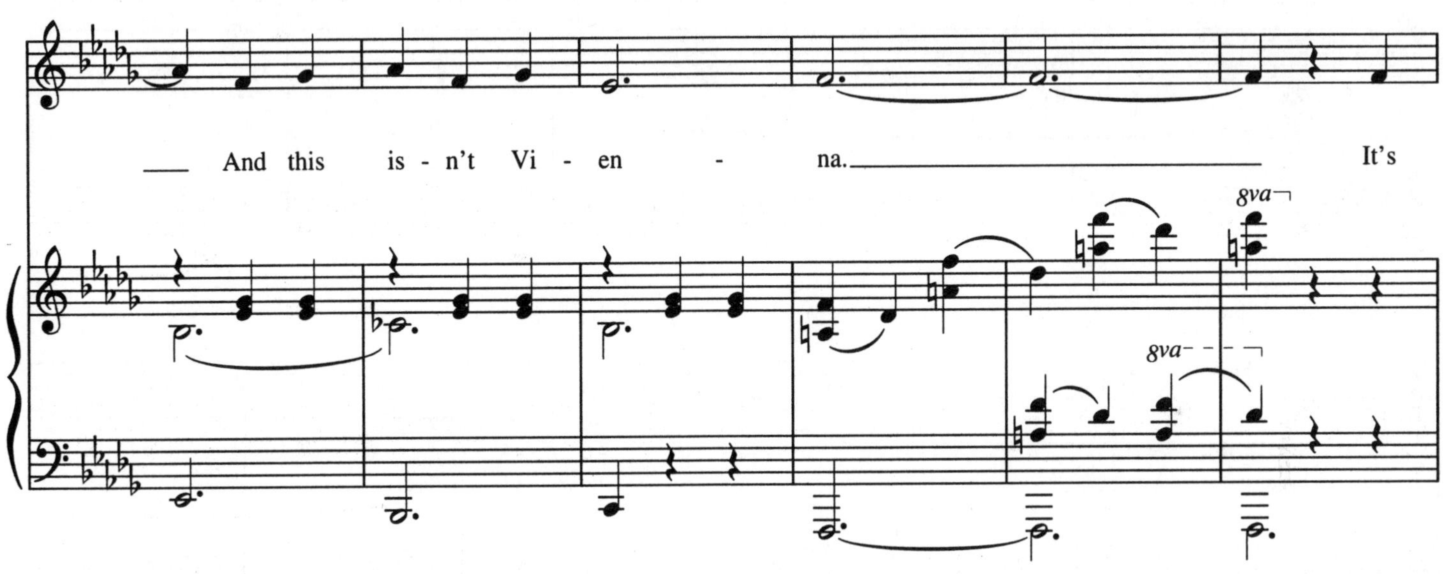
And this is - n't Vi - en - na.
It's
8va
8va

me, I sup - pose
Hold your hat, There it goes a -

gain, A con - tin - u - al waltz. It
seems to be real, But is it a
waltz Or just how I feel?
Pe - cu - liar if true, But the Dan - ube was nev - er so
L.H.
L.H.

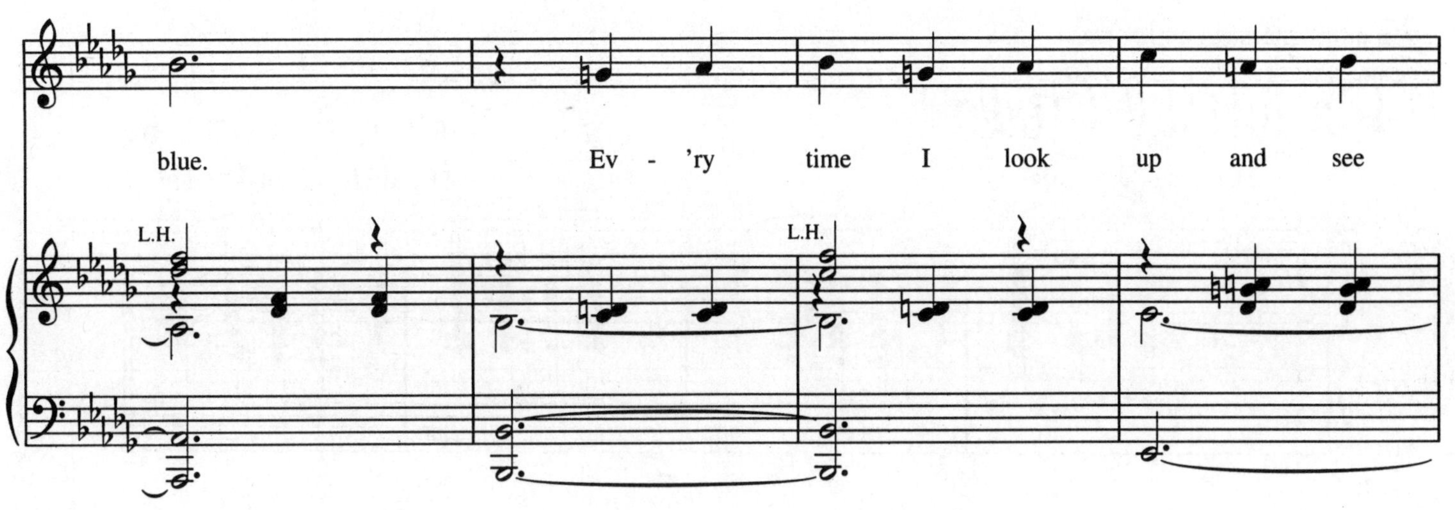
blue. Ev - 'ry time I look up and see
L.H.
L.H.

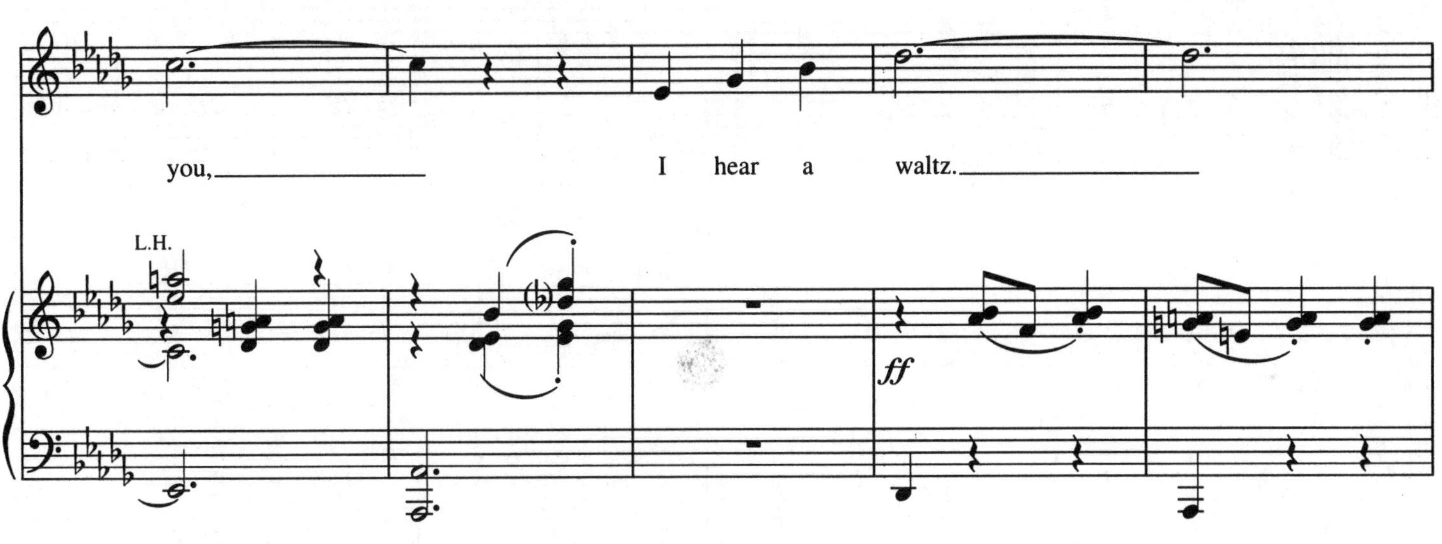
you, I hear a waltz.
L.H.
ff

8vb

From the Musical "Follies"

Beautiful Girls

Music and Lyrics by
Stephen Sondheim

Beautiful Girls - 3 - 1

© 1971 RANGE ROAD MUSIC, INC., QUARTET MUSIC, INC., RILTING MUSIC, INC. and BURTHEN MUSIC CO., INC.
All Rights Administered by CARLIN AMERICA, INC.
All Rights Reserved Used by Permission

Em7(–5)
A7
Dm11
No rose can com - pare,
You may lose con - trol.
Noth - ing re - spect - a - ble
Faced with these Lo - re - leis,
G7
G+
Cmaj9
C6
Cmaj9
C6
Half so de - lec - ta - ble.
What man can mor - al - ize?
Cheer them in their glo - ry,
Cau - tion, on your guard with
D13/9
D9
G11
G13/9
G11
F+11
Dia-monds and pearls,
Beau - ti - ful girls,
Dazz - ling jew - els by the
Flaw - less charm - ers ev - 'ry
Em7(–5)
(A bass)
Dm7
Dm9(–5)
score.
one.
This is what beau - ty can be,
This is how Sam - son was shorn:

C/G
Bb♭m/A♭
A7
Dm11
Dm7
G7
Beau - ty ce - les - tial, the best, you'll a - gree: All for you, these Beau - ti - ful
Each in her style a De - li - lah re - born, Each a gem, A beau - ti - ful
f
1. C
girls!
2. Em7–5
A7
Dm11
Dm7
G7
ten. G9
di - a - dem of beau - ti - ful - - Wel - come them, these Beau - ti - ful
ten.
cresc.
C
girls!
ff
gliss.

From the Musical "Merrily We Roll Along"

Growing Up

Music and Lyrics by
Stephen Sondheim

© 1991 RILTING MUSIC, INC.
All Rights Administered by WB MUSIC CORP.
International Copyright Secured All Rights Reserved

(whistle)
Keep re - mind - ing me . . .
(marcato)
cresc.
Frank's old friends_ al - ways seem_ to come through . . .
mf
cresc.
f
molto rall.
Frank will, too . . ._
a tempo
So, old friends,_ Now it's time_ to start
molto rall.
a tempo
mp
Grow-ing up.__
Tak - ing charge,- See - ing things_ as they

are.
Fac-ing facts,
Not es-cap-ing them,
Still with dreams,
Just re-shap-ing them.
Grow-ing up.
rall.
cresc.
rall.
Risoluto
Char-ley is a hot-head,
Char-ley won't budge.
mf
non legato
Char-ley is a friend.
p
mf
Char-ley is a scream-er,

Char - ley won't bend.
Char - ley's in your cor - ner.
Mar - y is a dream - er,
Mar - y's a friend.
Mar - y is a nudge.
Mar - y is a pur - ist,
Char - ley's a judge.
Char - ley is a drop - out,
Ev - 'ry - thing's a "cop - out."
Why is it old friends don't want old friends to

change?
mf legato
Ev - 'ry road has a turn - ing, That's the way you keep learn - ing:
dim.
rit.
a tempo (♩ = 𝅗𝅥)
So, old friends, Don't you see we can
a tempo
mf
have it all,
Mov - ing on, Get - ting out of the

past?
Solv - ing dreams,_ Not just trust - ing them,
Tak - ing dreams,_ Re - ad - just - ing them, Grow-ing up,
cresc.
Grow-ing up.
dim.
Grow - ing up,___ Be - ing flex - i - ble,
mf
Bend-ing with_ the road,_
Add - ing dreams_ When the oth - ers don't

last.
Grow-ing up,
Un-der - stand - ing that
grow-ing nev - er ends.
Like old dreams,
Some old dreams,
Like old friends.
mp
dim.
p
(whistle)
p
ten.
(whistle)
ten.
ten.
f
6

From "Kukla, Fran And Ollie"

The Two Of You

Music and Lyrics by
Stephen Sondheim

Moderato

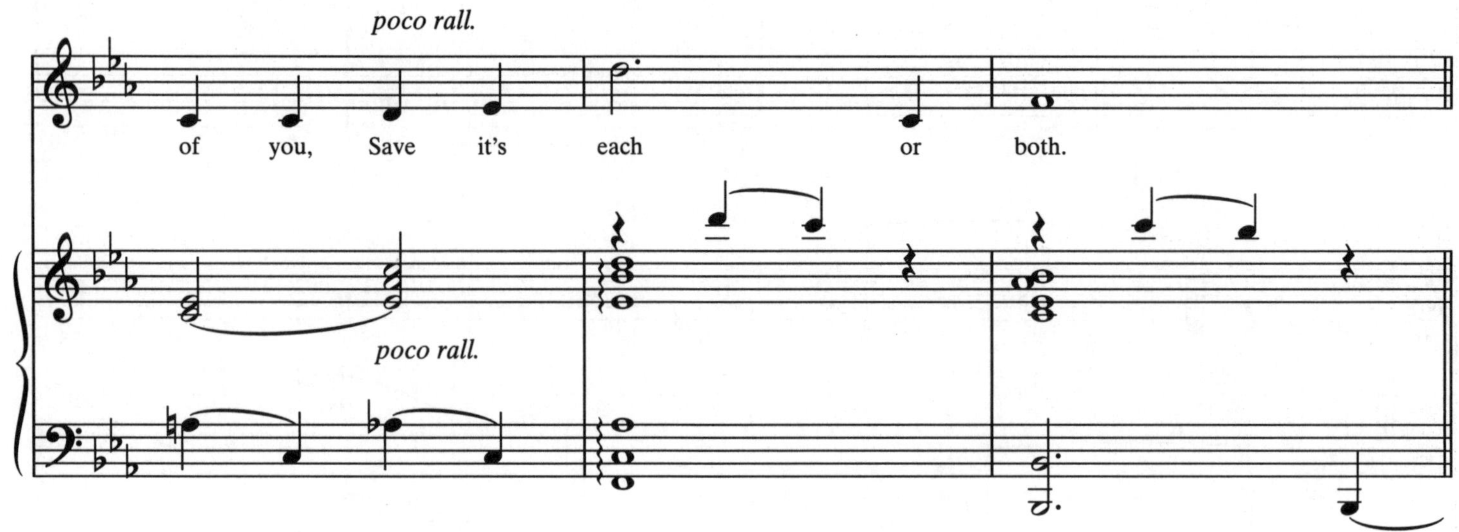

© 1955 (Unpublished) Chappell & Co. (Renewed)
© 1999 RILTING MUSIC, INC.
All Rights Administererd by WB MUSIC CORP.
All Rights Reserved

Slowly, freely
Ev' - ry - day I think a - new of you,
How I love the
two of you.
And I fond - ly hope the two of you do,
too.
Dope that I
am,
I can't think what to say,
Just
mp
poco cresc.
mf

"Hope cake and jam and Hap - pi - ness
dim. poco
(♭)
come your way."
I want no one else in lieu of you;
mp
(♮)
I pre - fer the two of you.
And I'd like to take the
cresc.
two of you to tea.

Come spend the day; Oh, what love - ly sights we'll
mf
see! But noth - ing's sweet - er than The
mp
ten.
view of you, So stay, the two of you, with
ten.
ten.
me.

From the Musical "Into The Woods"

Giants In The Sky

Music and Lyrics by
Stephen Sondheim

Andante moderato, non rubato (♩ = 132)

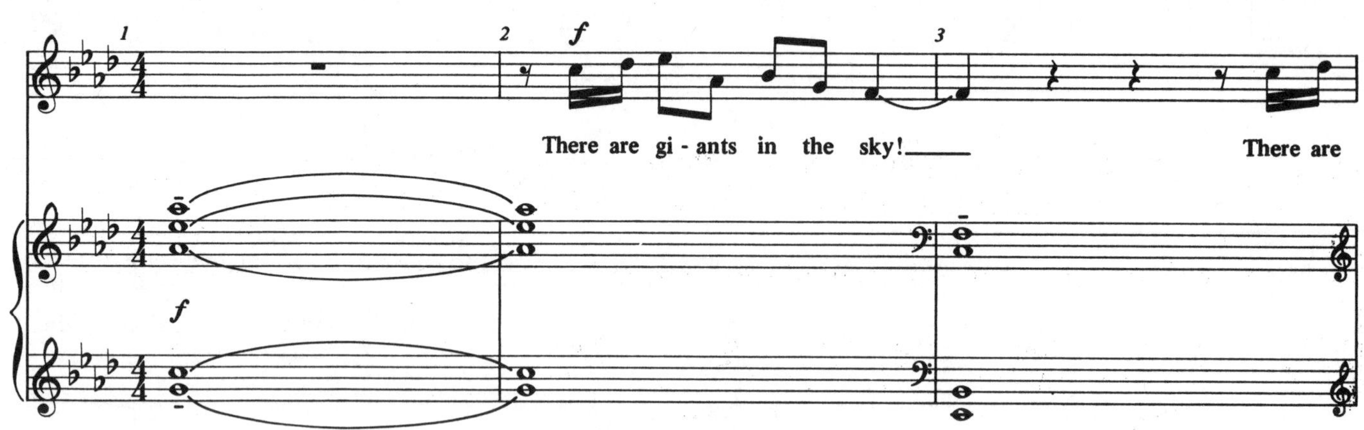

© 1987 RILTING MUSIC, INC.
All Rights Administered by WB MUSIC CORP.
International Copyright Secured All Rights Reserved

10
11
12
J.
more than a glance is e - nough to show you Just how small you are.
When you're
cresc.
13
To→15
16
way up high and you're on your own In a world like none that you've ev-er known, Where the sky is lead and the earth is stone, You're
mp non legato
mf
17
18
free to do What - ev - er pleas - es you, Ex -
19
20
plor - ing things you'd nev - er dare 'Cause you don't care, When sud - den - ly there's a

Broadly
J.
Big tall ter-ri-ble gi - ant at the door,
mf
mf legato
A big tall ter-ri-ble la - dy gi - ant,
sweep-ing the floor.
And she gives you food and she gives

30
31
32
mp
J.
— you rest — And she draws you close to her gi - ant breast, — And you
33
34
35
know things now that you nev - er knew be - fore,
mp
36
37
38
Not till the sky. —
On-ly
p non legato, marcato
39
40
41
cresc.
just when you've made a friend and all, And you know she's big but you don't feel small, Some-one big-ger than her comes a-long the hall To

J.
swal - low you for lunch.
And your
heart is lead and your stom-ach stone And you're
poco cresc.
mp legato e misterioso
real - ly scared be-ing all a-lone. . .
And it's
then that you long for the things you've known And the
dim.
p
cresc.
world you've left and the lit - tle you own- -The
fun
is done.
You
steal what you can and run!
And you
poco cresc.
sub. mf
scram - ble down and you look
be - low
And the
world you
know
be - gins
to
grow: The
cresc.

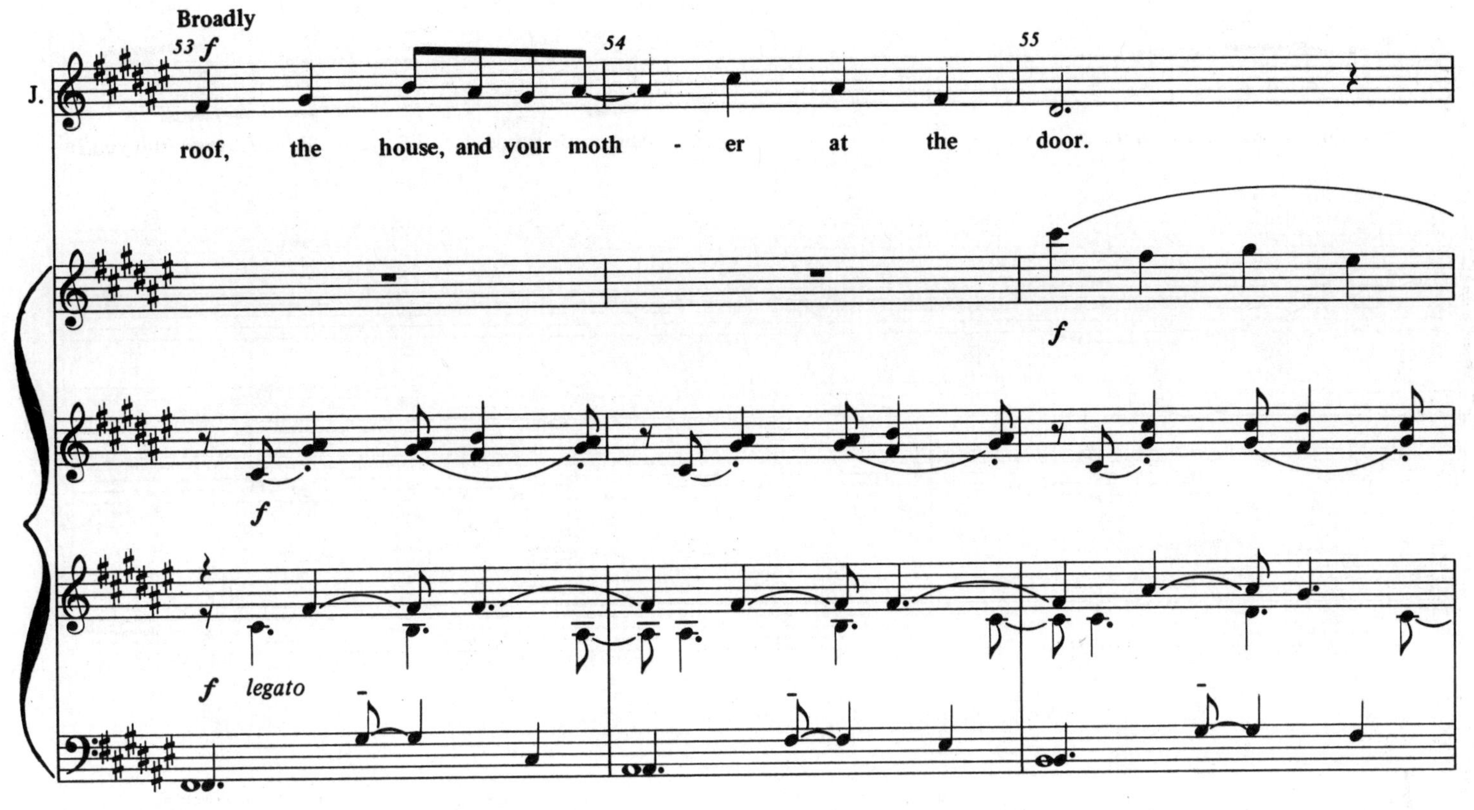
Broadly
53
54
55
J.
roof, the house, and your moth - er at the door.
f
f
f legato

56
57
58
J.
The roof, the house, and the world___ you nev - er

59
60
61
J.
thought to ex - plore.
And you think of all of the things
62
63
64
mf
you've seen,
And you wish that you could live in be - tween,
And you're
dim.
65
66
67
back a - gain, on - ly dif - f'rent than be - fore,
mf

J.
(Intensely)
mp
After the sky.
There are
f
giants in the sky!
cresc.
There are big tall terrible awesome scary
mf
cresc.
wonderful giants
In the sky!

From the Motion Picture "Stavisky"

Theme From "Stavisky"

Music by Stephen Sondheim

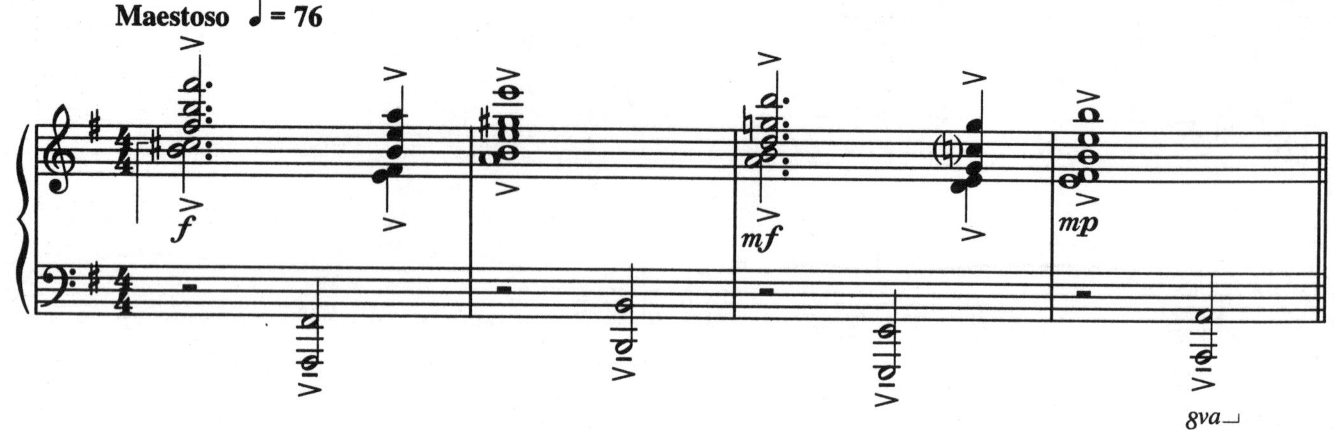

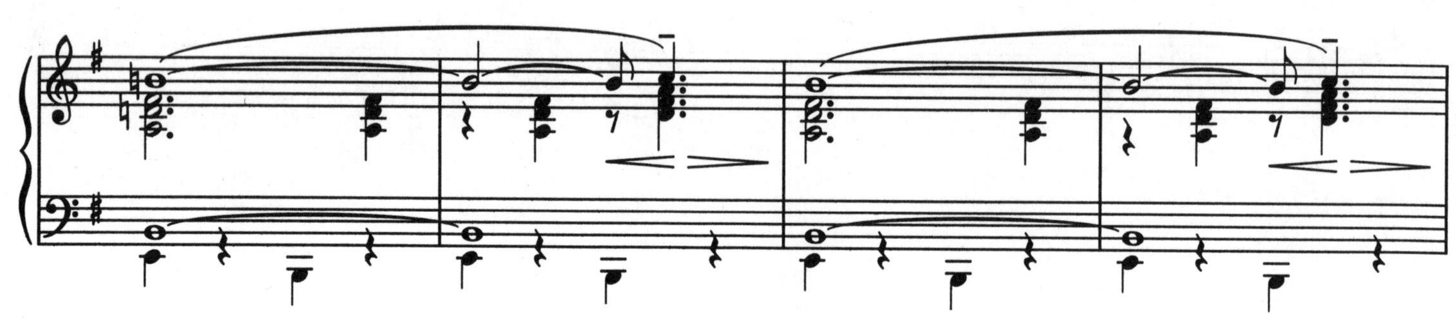

© 1975, 1997 PEMA MUSIC/CAMCINE TV MUSIC, INC.
All Rights Reserved Used by Permission

mf
dim.
p

poco dim.
marcato
r.h.
mp
Emphasize the melody
mp legato

f
f
dim. poco a poco
dim. poco a poco

mp
mp
dim.
Maestoso ♩ = 76
f
mf
mp
p
8va

From the Musical "Passion"

Happiness

(Solo Version)

Music and Lyrics by
Stephen Sondheim

Adagio (♩ = 124)

© 1994 by RILTING MUSIC, INC. (ASCAP)
This Version © 1997 by RILTING MUSIC, INC. (ASCAP)
All Rights Throughout the World Administered by WB MUSIC CORP.
All Rights Reserved including Public Performance for Profit

3
this right now, Here in your arms?
That we ev - er should have
cresc.
met is a mir - a - cle.
No, in - ev - i - ta - ble.
In - ev - i - ta - ble,
mf
molto legato
yes, But I con - fess It was the
look, That look, The sad - ness in your
eyes That day when we glanced at each oth - er in the park.
We saw that we were
cresc.
mf grazioso

both un - hap - py. I pit - ied you, you pit - ied me. How quick-ly pit - y leads to
dim.
Tranquillo
poco rall.
a tempo
poco rall.
love.
All this
mp
poco rall.
a tempo
poco rall.
a tempo
hap - pi - ness,
Mere-ly from a glance in the park.
a tempo
So much hap - pi - ness,
So much

love.
I thought I knew what
cresc.
love was.
I wish we could have
sub. mp
met so much soon - er.
I thought I knew what
marc.
love was.
I thought I knew how

much I could feel.
I did - n't know what love was,
mf
But now I do.
poco rall.
It's what I feel with
cresc.
f
poco rall.
a tempo
you,
The hap - pi - ness I
a tempo
risoluto
poco rall.
feel with you.
So much
poco rall.

Rubato

hap - pi - ness Hap-pen - ing by chance in a park.

(*f*) *mf*

Sure - ly this is hap - pi - ness No one else has

f

ev - er felt be - fore.______ Just an - oth - er

poco dim.

An - oth - er sim - ple love sto - ry,
Are - n't all of them the
dim.
poco rall.
Poco rubato
same?
No, but this is more,
more, We feel
poco rall.
mp
more, This is so much more
Like ev - 'ry oth - er
cresc.
a tempo
love sto - ry.
Some say
mp
a tempo

a tempo
hap - pi - ness
comes and goes.
mf molto espress.
a tempo
mp
Then this hap - pi - ness is a kind of hap - pi - ness No one real - ly
cresc.
knows.
I did - n't know what
mf
love was.
I thought it was no more than a name for
poco rit.
poco rit.

a tempo
yearn - ing. I thought is was what kind - ness be - came. I'm
a tempo
mp
poco rit.
rall.
learn - ing. I thought where there was love there was shame.
But with you there's just
poco rit.
rall.
dim.
a tempo
hap - pi - ness . . .
End - less
a tempo
p
(1st time only)
Repeat and fade
hap - pi - ness . . .
dim. poco a poco

From the Television Production "Evening Primrose"

If You Can Find Me, I'm Here

Music and Lyrics by
Stephen Sondheim

© 1966 (Renewed 1994) Stephen Sondheim,
BURTHEN MUSIC COMPANY, INC., Owner of Publication and Allied Rights for the World
CHAPPELL & CO., Sole Selling Agent
All Rights Reserved Used by Permission

done. They're gone. I am a gen - ius. Charles, you are an
un - a - dul - ter - at - ed gen - ius, You are an in - dis - put - a - bly ex - traor - di - nar - y... What was
accel. molto
rit.
that? Not a thing.
accel. molto
cresc.
rit.
dim.
a tempo
You're a fool. You are a - lone.
a tempo

And it be - gins.
Care - ful.
Care - ful.
Must-n't get ex - cit - ed, Must-n't o - ver - do it.
Soft - ly.
Tip - toe.
You'll get used to it in no time.
Look at it!
Beau - ti - ful!

What a place to live, What a place to write! I shall be in-spir-ed, I shall turn out
el-e-gies and son-nets, Vers-es by the ton. At last I have a home, And
no-bod-y will know, No one in the world, No-bod-y will know I'm here!
I am free! I am free!

Good - bye, my
sim.
p
friends, and good rid - dance.
Par - don while
I dis - ap - pear.
Come see me
soon in my hide - a - way.
If you can

find me, I'm here.
Fare - well, you
blood - suck - ing land - lords,
Pour - ing your
sim.
threats in my ear.
Good luck for -
ev - er to you and yours.
If you can

find me, I'm here.
And I'll stay,
legato
Co - zi - ly hid - ing by day.
Dur - ing the day I'll re - sign,

Wait - ing till you go a - way.
But at nine,
Mas - ter of all I sur - vey,
Ev - 'ry - thing gets to be Mine to own,

Mine to use, Mine to
write All the po - ems I choose,
All a - lone, On - ly me and my muse And
for - ty pi - an - os And ten thou - sand shoes.

p
sim.
Fare - well, Ne - an - der - thal neigh - bors,
p
Swill - ing your pret - zels and beer.
Fair weath - er friends, do you miss me now?

If you can find me, I'm here.
Good - bye, de - spoil - ers of beau - ty.
p
sim.
Ru - in an - oth - er ca - reer.
When you wake up with one gen - ius less,

If you can find me, I'm here!
And I'm free,
legato
Free as a bird in a tree,
Free as the slip - pers I wear,

Free with a year's war - ran - tee.
Free as air,
All of these prod - ucts and me.
All that I ask is a chair that tilts,

Books to read, Light re - fresh - ment be - fore I pro - ceed.
And a blaz - er Or may - be a tweed, The bar - est es - sen - tials a po - et would need.

sim.
Live in your bar - bar - ous jun - gle,
Scream - ing for ways to get clear.
When all the scream - ing has died a - way,

Come and vis - it my hide - a -
way. I will be glad to pro -
vide a way. If you can
sub. p
find me, I'm
gliss.

here!
I am
here!
I am
here!
I am
here!
I am
here!
I am...

From the T V Musical "I Believe In You"

They Ask Me Why I Believe In You

Music and Lyrics by
Stephen Sondheim

© 1990 RILTING MUSIC, INC.
All Rights Administered by WB MUSIC CORP.
All Rights Reserved

mp
blind Or I'm out of my mind.
legato
mp
They'd be star-tled to find Ev-'ry word is true.
dim.
p
They ask me why I be-lieve in you.
p
poco cresc.
I on-ly re-ply I be-lieve in you.
poco cresc.

mf
So, dar - ling, if you don't think half e - nough
mf legato
of your - self, It's be - cause you don't love your - self As I
dim.
poco rall.
To Coda
p a tempo
do.
rall.
D.S. al
Take heart, my
Coda
do.

From the Musical "Saturday Night"

I Remember That

Music and Lyrics by
Stephen Sondheim

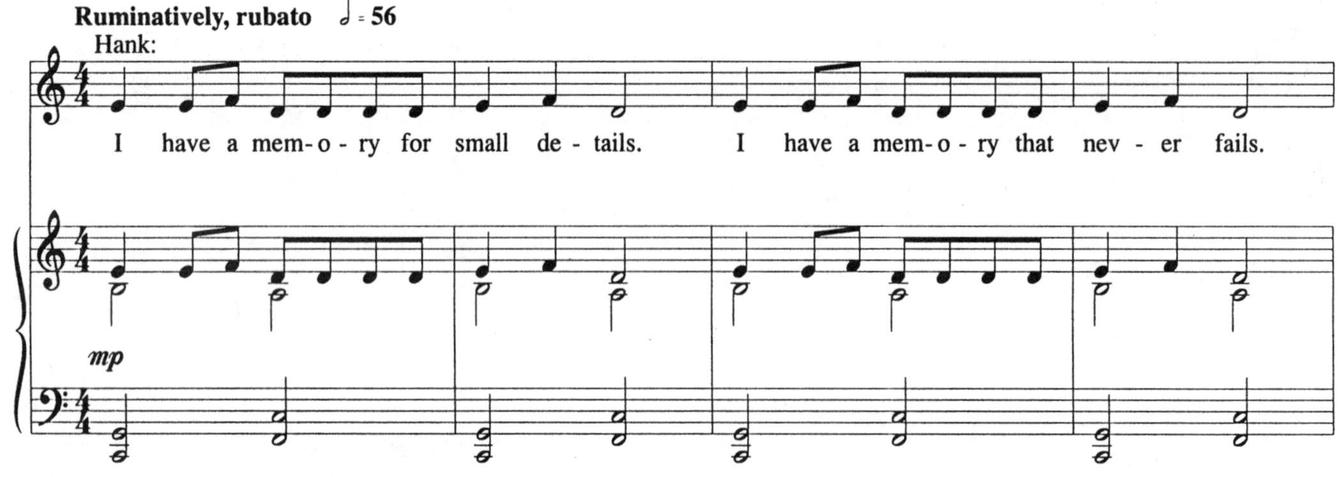

© 1998 BURTHEN MUSIC COMPANY, INC.
All Rights Administered by CHAPPELL & CO.
International Copyright Secured All Rights Reserved

haz - y on: That was the date we had, I re-mem - ber, in ear - ly Sep-tem - ber, Or
was it No-vem - ber, three years a - go? Up to a cer - tain point my mind is
rit.
clear. Ev - 'ry de-tail of that date that fate - ful
rit.
Even rhythm
year. I ar-rived at sev - en;

I'd stopped a - long the way
To buy a big bou - quet for you. I re - mem - ber
that.
In a French - type rest - 'rant,
Run by a guy named Jake,
We had a sir - loin steak for two. I re - mem - ber that.
L.H.
I re - mem - ber we
sat out in Pros - pect Park in the glow of moon - light.
Af - ter that, we went back to
mf

your house and danced till dawn. I was pour-ing cof-fee, You lit a cig - a-
rette. From then on I for - get What I said, What I did and where I was at!
For I'd fal - len in love with you, I re-mem-ber I'd fal - len in love with
you, That's the one thing I do re-mem - ber, I re-mem-ber that.
f
mp

Celeste:
Up to a point your mind is clear, no doubt.
But I can re-mem-ber some
mf
dim.
things that you left out.
I was dressed at
mp
sev - en,
But you ar-rived at eight.
And you were nev - er
late a - gain.
I re-mem - ber that.
Since you'd bought me

flow - ers,
You could-n't pay
the check.
You were a ner - vous
wreck
by then.
I re-mem-ber that.
L.H.
I re-mem-ber we
sat in the park In the glow of a p'lice-man's flash - light.
Af - ter
mf
that we went back to my house and sat some more.
You were pour - ing

cof - fee
All ov - er my new dress.
From then on I con -
fess I for - get What I said and where I was at!
rall.
But I
f
rall.
a tempo
did fall in love with you, I re - mem - ber I did fall in love with you, That's the one thing I
a tempo
mp
do re - mem - ber, I re - mem - ber that.
rit.
8vb

Cut from the Musical "Follies"

That Old Piano Roll

Music and Lyrics by
Stephen Sondheim

© 1971 RANGE ROAD MUSIC, INC., QUARTET MUSIC, INC., RILTING MUSIC, INC. and BURTHEN MUSIC CO., INC.
All Rights Administered by CARLIN AMERICA, INC.
All Rights Reserved Used by Permission

I just got - ta dance, And what I mean is
dance with you.
Does - n't mat - ter what I'm do - ing or where.
When that rag - time rhy - thm tick - les the air,

I go in a trance.
I on - ly wan-na dance with
you.
8va
3
3
3
3
Ba - by,
p legato
Ba - by, Come on a - long, Come on and dance, And
stacc. e cresc.

may - be
legato
By the time you get a load - a that Su - per syn - co - pa - ted co - da, You'll
f
say, "I think that old pi - a - no roll's nice."
staccato
Then we'll play that old pi - a - no roll twice.

Come on, take a chance,
I on - ly wan-na dance with
you!
8va
mp marcato
There's a honk - y-tonk down the street,
Noth - in' more_ than a dive.
They got some-thin', though, can't be beat,
Some - thin' real - ly a - live: They got this

play-er pi - a - no, It's noth - in' but a pi - a - no. Yeah - bo, But
legato
what a pi - a - no! The on - ly tune that it has is jazz. It's just a
mi - ni pi - a - no, A ti - ny, tin - nu pi - a - no, But folks from
ev - 'ry cit - y, town and ghet - to A - dore that ad lib. al - le - gret - to. Just
f

lis - ten to that old pi - a - no roll play.
staccato
I could hear that old pi - a - no all day.
I just wan-na dance, And what I mean is dance with
you.
Makes no diff - 'rence,
staccato

Sun - ny weath - er or rain,
When that rag - time rhy - thm reach - es my brain.
I know in ad - vance I'm gon - na wan-na dance with you!
3

Ba
-
by,
Ba
-
by, Kick out the blues, Kick off your shoes. And may
-
p
legato
stacc. e cresc.
legato

be
That sym - pa - thet - ic
f

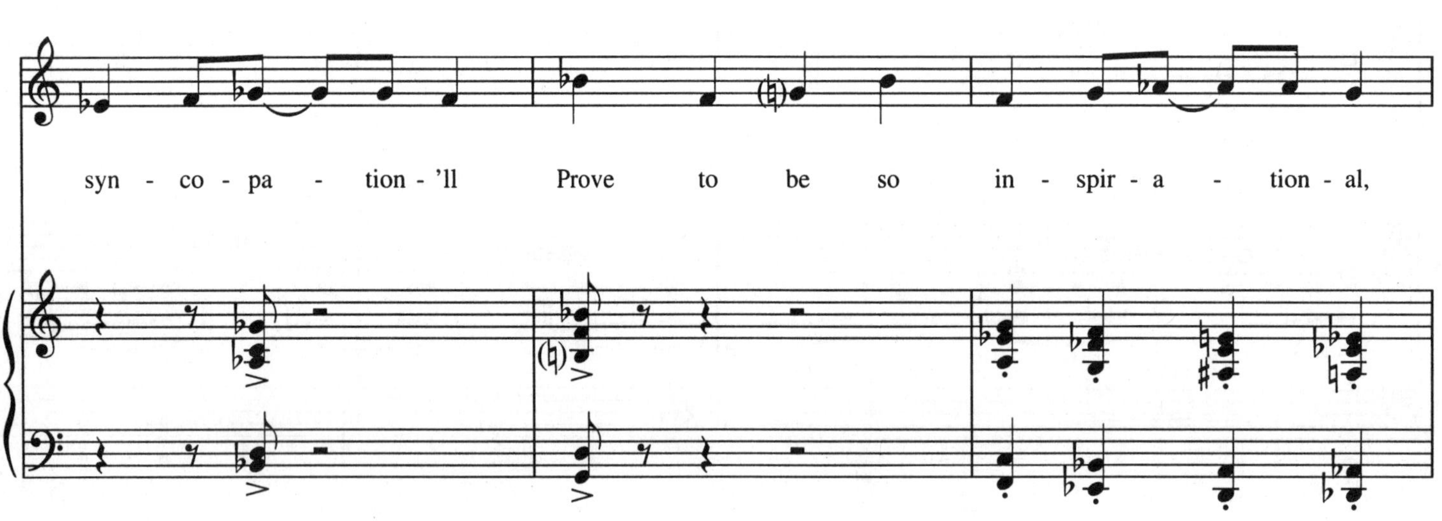
syn - co - pa - tion - 'll Prove to be so in - spir - a - tion - al,

We won't let that old pi - a - no roll stop.
staccato

We'll keep drop-pin' nick-els in till we drop.

I don't want ro - mance,
I on-ly wan-na dance with . . .

I just wan-na . . . I just got-ta . . . I just wan-na . . . Dance!
sfz

From the Musical "Anyone Can Whistle"

With So Little To Be Sure Of

Music and Lyrics by
Stephen Sondheim

Moderato

Piano

mf tranquillo

REFRAIN *(with some freedom)*

Em A7sus Dm7 G7

With so lit - tle to be sure of,

mp

C A7sus A7 Dm7 Em7

If there's an - y - thing at all,________ If there's

Am Bb7 G7sus G7 Em A7-5

an - y - thing at all, I'm sure of here and now and

© 1964 Stephen Sondheim
BURTHEN MUSIC COMPANY, INC., Owner of Publication and Allied Rights throughout the World.
CHAPPELL & CO., Administrator
International Copyright Secured All Rights Reserved
Unauthorized copying, arranging, adapting, recording or public performance is an infringement of Copyright.
Infringers are liable under the law.

Ab6
G7
Em
A7sus
Dm7
us to - geth - er. All I'll - ev - er be I owe
mf
mp
G7
C
A7sus
A7
Dm7
you, If there's an - y - thing to be.
C
Am
Dm
Dm7
G7
Bm7
Be - ing sure e - nough of you makes me sure e - nough of me.
mf
E7
Gm7
C9
Thanks for ev - 'ry - thing we did, Ev - ry - thing that's
p

F6
Am7
C7
C9
F6/9
past, Ev'-ry-thing that's o - ver too fast.
mf
F6
Bbmaj7
Em7
None of it was wast - ed, All of it will last,
dim.
A7
Am7
C7
D9
G11
G13
Ev'-ry-thing that's here and now and us to - geth - er!
cresc.
Em
A7sus
Dm7
G7
C
It was mar - vel-ous to know you And it
mf

A7sus
A7
Dm7
Em7
C
Am
G7sus
is - n't real - ly through.
Cra - zy bus-'ness this, this life we
espressivo
G7
Em7
C
Am
G7sus
G7
Em7
C
live in. Can't com - plain a - bout the time we're giv - en! With so
Am
Dm7
1.
G7
D
(C bass)
C
Gm7
G7 -9 +5
lit - tle to be sure of in this world, we had a mo - ment.
rit.
sub. p
2.
G11
D
(C bass)
C
D
(C bass)
C
world, hold me. Hold me.
sub. p

From the Musical "Saturday Night"

Saturday Night

Music and Lyrics by
Stephen Sondheim

© 1983 BURTHEN MUSIC COMPANY, INC.
All Rights Administered by CHAPPELL & CO.
All Rights Reserved

(Dialogue)
Artie:
pit - cha?
Cush- man.
How does the com - bi -
So when I got my
na - tion of
mind on sex,
John - ny Mack Brown and
Who gives a damn for
Bess - ie Love
Fran - cis X.
hit - cha?
Bush- man?
(Dialogue)
legato
Dino:
The moon's like a
The moon's like an
mil - lion watt e - lec - tric
ov - er - load - ed Mox - ie
light
sign,
It shines up the ci - ty as it climbs.
It shines at you friend - ly and bright.
And

I've got-ta spend an-oth-er Sat-ur-day night At home with the New York Times.
I got my bud-dies and my bud-dies are fine But not on a Sat-ur-day night!
staccato
To Coda
Ted:
Moon-light on Flat-bush A-ve-nue That's what I call a love-ly view.
mp
Tempo I
f
rall.
Poco meno mosso
Easy
mp
Dino:
(2nd time)
So

what can you do on a Sat-ur-day night a-lone?
Who needs a view on a Sat-ur-day night a-lone?
If it's a Sat-ur-day night and you are sin-gle,
You sit with a pa-per and fight the urge to min-gle.
And home is a place where you got-ta go back a-lone.

Home is a place where the fu-ture looks black, a - lone.
I like the Sun-day Times all right, but not in bed. A - live and a-lone on a
Sat-ur-day night is dead!
D.C. al Coda
CODA
Ray:
Johnny Mack Brown and Bess - ie Love.
Ted: Love...
Artie: Love...
Dino: Love...
Ray: Love...
mp
Ted: Love...
Artie: Love...
Dino: Love...
Ray: Love...
Ted: Love...
Artie: Love...
Dino: Love...
Ray: So

Ray:
what can you do on a Sat-ur-day night a - lone?
Ted:
What can you do on a Sat-ur-day night a - lone?
Artie:
What can you do on a Sat-ur-day night
Dino:
What can you do on a
Who needs a view on a Sat-ur-day night a - lone?
Who needs a view on a Sat-ur-day night a - lone?
a - lone? Who needs a view on a Sat-ur-day night
Sat-ur-day night a - lone? Who needs a view on a

If it's a Sat-ur-day night and you are sin - gle, You
If it's a Sat-ur-day sin - gle, You
a - lone? Sin - gle, You
Sat-ur-day night a - lone? Sin - gle, You
mf
8vb
sit with a pa-per and fight the urge to min - gle. And
sit with a pa-per and fight the urge to min - gle.
sit with a pa-per and fight the urge to min - gle.
sit with a pa-per and fight the urge to min - gle.
p

home is a place where you got-ta go back a - lone.
Home is a place where you got-ta go back a - lone.
Home is a place where you got-ta go back
Home is a place where you
mp
Home is a place where the fu-ture looks black, a - lone.
Home is a place where the fu-ture looks black, a - lone.
a - lone. Home is a place where the fu-ture looks black, a -
got-ta go back a - lone. Home is a place where

Thing's-'d be diff-'rent an-y oth-er night in-stead, But we're on our own on a
Thing's-'d be diff-'rent an-y oth-er night in-stead, But we're on our own on a
lone. Diff-'rent an-y oth-er night in-stead, But we're on our own on a
thing's-'d be diff-'rent an-y oth-er night in-stead, But we're on our own on a
mf
All:
Sat-ur-day night, With no one to phone on a Sat-ur-day night,
And when you're a-lone on a Sat-ur-day night,
cresc.

— You might as well be dead!
(Orchestra)
f
ff detache
Dino:
(with his elbow)

From the Motion Picture "Dick Tracy"

What Can You Lose?

Music and Lyrics by
Stephen Sondheim

Lazy Blues (♩ = 108)

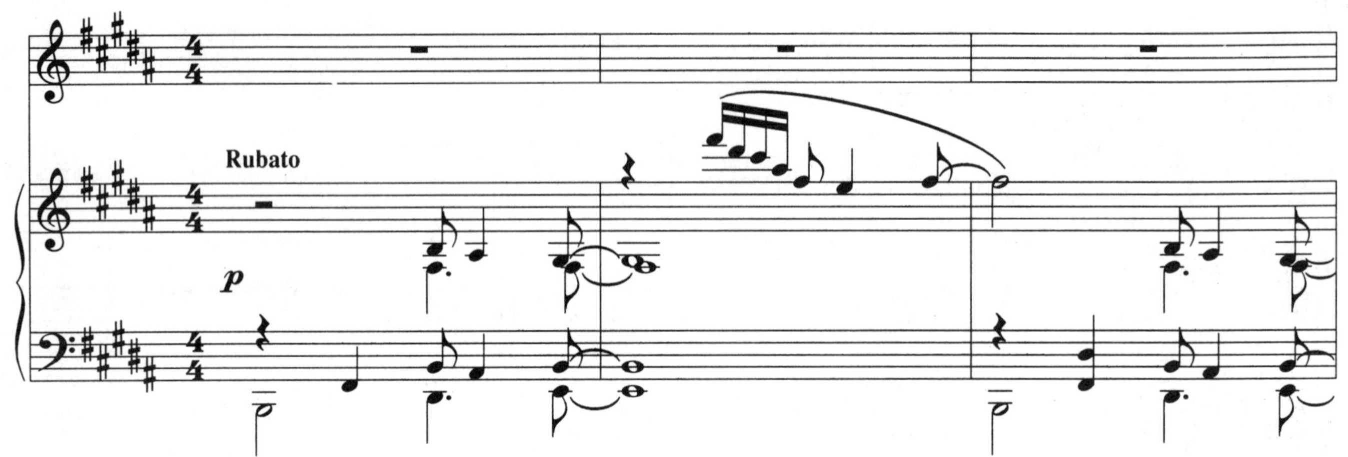

© 1990 RILTING MUSIC, INC. and TOUCHSTONE PICTURES MUSIC & SONGS, INC.
All Rights on behalf of RILTING MUSIC, INC. Administered by WB MUSIC CORP.
All Rights Reserved

feel - ing? Say it to her - - What can you lose? May - be it shows,
She's had clues, which she chose to ig - nore.
poco cresc.
p
May - be, though, she knows, And just wants to go on as be- fore.
dim.
p
cresc.
mp
As a friend, nothing more.
p
mp

So she clos - es the door.
Well, if she does,
p
mp
sub. mf
Those are the dues.
mp
Once the words are spo - ken, Some - thing may be bro - ken. Still, you love her - -
cresc. poco a poco
What can you lose?
But what if she goes?
At least now,
mf
poco dim
p
poco cresc.

(ten.)
you have part of her. What if she had to choose? Leave it a - lone.
(ten.)
dim.
sub.
mp
p
mp
Hold it all in.
cresc.
Bet - ter a bone. Don't ev - en be - gin. With so much to
mf
Rall.
win, There's too much to lose.
mp
Rall. . .
p

From the Musical "Follies"

The Story Of Lucy And Jessie

Music and Lyrics by
Stephen Sondheim

© 1971 RANGE ROAD MUSIC, INC., QUARTET MUSIC, INC., RILTING MUSIC, INC. and BURTHEN MUSIC CO., INC.
All Rights Administered by CARLIN AMERICA, INC.
All Rights Reserved Used by Permission

Let us call them Lu - cy "X" and Jes - sie "Y", which are
not their re - al names.
Now Lu - cy has the pur - i - ty, A -
long with the un - sur - e - ty, That comes with be - ing on - ly twen - ty - one.
Jes - sie has ma - tur - i - ty And plen - ty of se - cu - ri - ty. What -

ev - er you can do with them, She's done.
Giv - en their ad - van - ta - ges, You may ask why the two
la - dies have such grief.
This is my be - lief,
In brief:

f
Lu - cy is juic - y, but ter - ri - bly drab.
mf
Jes - sie is dress - y, but cold as a slab.
Lu - cy wants to be dress - y,
Jes - sie wants to be juic - y.

Lu - cy wants to be Jes - sie And Jes - sie Lu - cy. You see,
Jes - sie is rac - y, but hard as a rock.
Lu - cy is lac - y, but dull as a smock.
Jes - sie wants to be lac - y, Lu - cy wants to be Jes - sie.

That's the sor - row - ful pré - cis, It's ver - y mess - y.
f
f
Poor sad souls,
itch - ing to be switch - ing roles.

Lu - cy wants to do what
Jes - sie does.
mf
Jes - sie wants to be what Lu - cy was.
f

Lu - cy's a lass - ie you pat on the head.
mf
Jes - sie is class - y but vir - tu'l - ly dead.
Lu - cy wants to be class - y, Jes - sie wants to be Lass - ie. If
Lu - cy and Jes - sie could on - ly com - bine,
cresc.

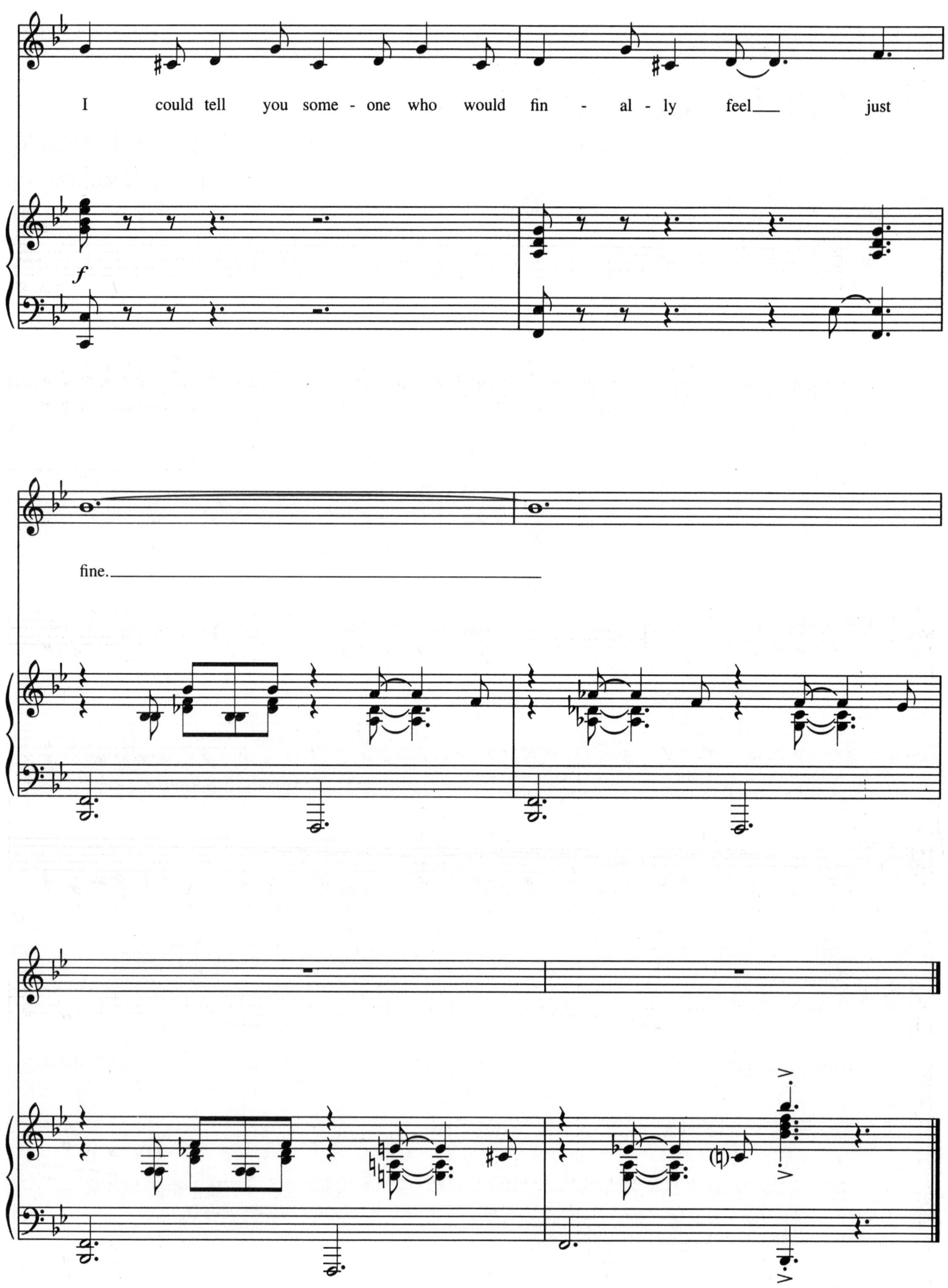
I could tell you some - one who would fin - al - ly feel just
f
fine.

Cut From the Musical "Follies"

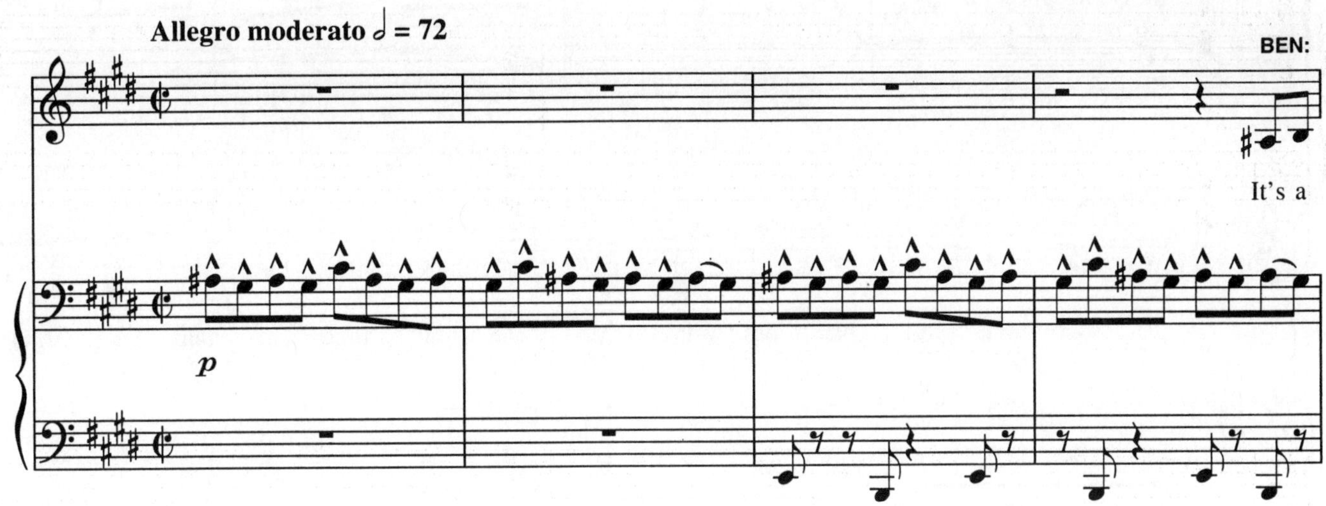

Pleasant Little Kingdom

Music and Lyrics by
Stephen Sondheim

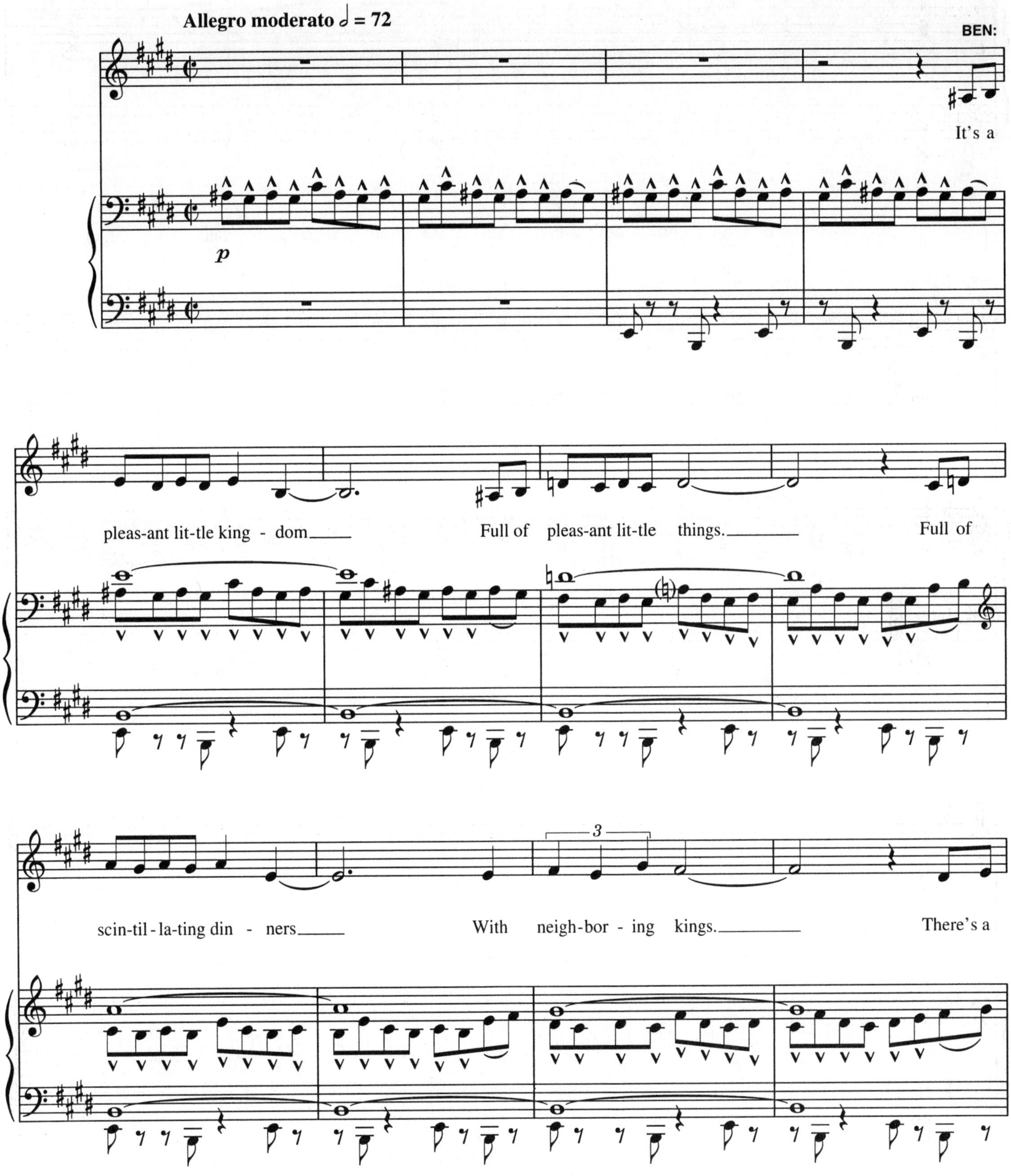
Allegro moderato ♩ = 72
BEN:
It's a
pleas-ant lit-tle king - dom
Full of pleas-ant lit-tle things.
Full of
scin-til-la-ting din - ners
With neigh-bor - ing kings.
There's a
3
p

© 1971 RANGE ROAD MUSIC, INC., QUARTET MUSIC, INC., RILTING MUSIC, INC. and BURTHEN MUSIC CO., INC.
All Rights Administered by CARLIN AMERICA, INC.
All Rights Reserved Used by Permission

cas-tle in the coun - try
For week-ends of rest.
And we
en - ter - tain at par - ties In the lit - tle time re - main - ing And we're
en - ter - tained by oth - ers And it's ver - y en - ter - tain-ing . . .
An ef -
fi - cient lit - tle king - dom,
The do - min-ion of the Queen.
Where at
cresc.

3
an-y giv-en mo - ment
The ash-trays are clean.
There are
cresc. poco
sub. p
3
man-y lit-tle bat - tles
Which nev - er are fought.
And
cresc. poco a poco
if on oc - ca - sion I think a - bout you,
It's a
f molto legato
dim. molto
pleas-ant lit - tle thought.
So I write an-oth-er book
And I
cresc. poco a poco

head an - oth - er drive And we take a trip we took And the
din - ner guests ar - rive. And un - less you real - ly look, You would think we were a - live, And . . .
God! . . .
ff
non legato
dim. poco a poco

SALLY:
It's a
pleas-ant lit-tle king - dom
Full of pleas-ant lit-tle days,
There are
char-i-ties and lec - tures
And flow-ers to raise.
There are

am - a-teur dra-mat - ics
And eve - nings of bridge.
And I
go to civ - ic lun-cheons when there's some-one to re-mind me And I stu - dy the pi - a - no And I
nev-er look be-hind me.
It's a mer - ry lit - tle king - dom
Full of
mer-ry lit-tle chores.
Lots of gar-den-ing and fix - ing,
All
cresc. poco

3
very - y out - doors.
In the drive-way is a sports car
sub. p
cresc. poco a poco
3
I should-n't have bought.
And
if on oc - ca - sion I think a - bout you,
I e -
f molto legato
dim. molto
lim - in - ate the thought.
So I
p

read a lit - tle here And I sew a lit - tle there And the
cresc. poco a poco
child-ren dis - ap - pear And the cas - tle needs re - pair And I
Broadly
BEN:
nev - er shed a tear And I nev - er turn a hair And... Ben! God help me,
ff

a tempo
Sal - ly, I've loved you all my life!
a tempo
marc.
f non marc.
mf marc.
molto rit.
mp non marc.
molto rit.
p

© 1971 RANGE ROAD MUSIC, INC., QUARTET MUSIC, INC., RILTING MUSIC, INC. and BURTHEN MUSIC CO., INC.
All Rights Administered by CARLIN AMERICA, INC.
All Rights Reserved Used by Permission

C♯7sus 4
F♯7sus4
F♯7
spent, So con - tent, Wast - ing time with you.
dim.
Bmaj9
B6
Bmaj9
F♯7sus 4
Too man-y morn - ings, Wish-ing that the room might be filled with you,
Too man-y morn- ings, Wast-ed in pre - tend - ing I reach for you.
mf
F♯9/B
C♯m11/F♯
Bmaj7+11
C♯m-9 +13
Morn - ing to morn - ing, Turn-ing in - to days. All the
How man - y morn - ings Are there still to come? How much
E♭7sus4
E♭7
A♭9+11
(A♭)
A♭maj7
C7 13 -5
rall.
days that I thought would nev-er end, All the
time can we hope that there will be? Not much
poco accel.

poco accel.
rall.
F7sus
F7
Bb
(C/Bb)
Bbmaj7
D7(+5)
nights with an-oth-er day to spend, All those
time, but it's time e-nough for me, If there's
a tempo
To Coda
(Gm7–5)
Gm7sus4(no 3rd)
F/C
times I'd look up to see (Sal-ly) stand-ing at the
time To look up and (Some-one)
f
C9sus4
C7
Fmaj9/6
door, (Sal-ly / Some-one) mov-ing to the bed, (Sal-ly / Some-one) rest-ing in my
C9sus4
Dbmaj9
Db6
Dbmaj9
Db6
arms With (her / his) head a-gainst my head.
sub. p

C♯7sus4
F♯7sus4
F♯7
cresc.
D.S. al Coda
(a tempo)
Coda
F/C
B♭/C
see
Sal - ly
Some-one
stand-ing at the
door,
moving to the
F°/C
bed,
rest-ing in my
arms,
Molto rubato
sub. p
with
her
his
head a-gainst my
head.
a tempo
f
ff
rit. e dim.
pp

From the Musical "Assassins"

Unworthy Of Your Love

Music and Lyrics by
Stephen Sondheim

Scene: The basement rec room in John Hinckley's house. ***(Hinckley picks up his guitar and accompanies himself)***

HINCKLEY: Love, John.

Moderato (♩ = 112)

HINCKLEY:

© 1990, 1992 RILTING MUSIC, INC.
All Rights Administered by WB MUSIC CORP.
All Rights Reserved

H.
sky,
Jo - die.
Tell me, Jo - die, how I can earn your
H.
love.
I would swim o - ceans, I would move moun - tains, I would do
mf
H.
an - y - thing for you.
What do you want me to do?
poco rall.
H.
I am un - worth - y of your love,
Jo-die, Jo - die,
mp a tempo

H.
Let_ me prove worth - y of your love.
cresc.
H.
Tell_ me how I can earn your love,_ Set me free.
mf
dim.
(Lights up on Lynette "Squeaky" Fromme)
H.
How_ can I turn your love to me?
mp
FROMME:
I am nothing, You are wind and dev - il and
mp

F.
god,
Char-lie,
Take my blood and my bod - y for your
F.
love.
Let me feel fire,
Let me drink poi - son, Tell me to
mf
F.
tear my heart in two,
If that's what you want me to do....
p
poco rall.
F
I am un - worth - y of your love,
Char - lie, dar - lin',
mp

F.
I — have done noth - ing for your love. —
cresc.
F.
Let — me be worth - y of your love, — Set you free - -
mf
dim.
F.
I — would come take you from your
HINCKLEY:
I — would come take you from your life...
mp cresc. poco a poco

F.
H.
cell...
I — would crawl bel - ly - deep through
You would be queen to me, not wife...
Hell...
Ba - by, I'd die for you,
E - ven though I will al - ways
Ba - by, I'd die for you... —
E - ven though — I will al - ways
mf
know: —
I — am un - worth - y of your
cresc.
sub. mp

F.
H.
love,
Char - lie,
dar
-
lin',
Let_ me prove worth - y of your
love,
Jo - die,
dar
-
lin',
Let_ me prove worth - y of your
cresc.
love. ___
I'll_ find a way to earn your
love. ___
I'll_ find a way to earn your
f
love,_ Wait and see.
Then_ you will turn your love to
love, Wait and see.
Then_ you will turn your love to
dim.
mf

F.
me,
Your
H.
me,
Your
mp
F.
love
To
H.
love
To
dim. poco a poco
F.
me...
H.
me...
p
pp

From the Musical "Pacific Overtures"

There Is No Other Way

Music and Lyrics by
Stephen Sondheim

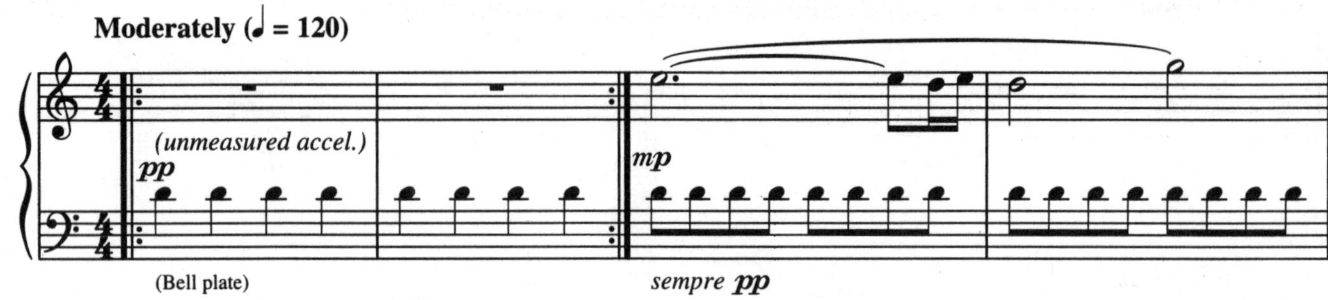

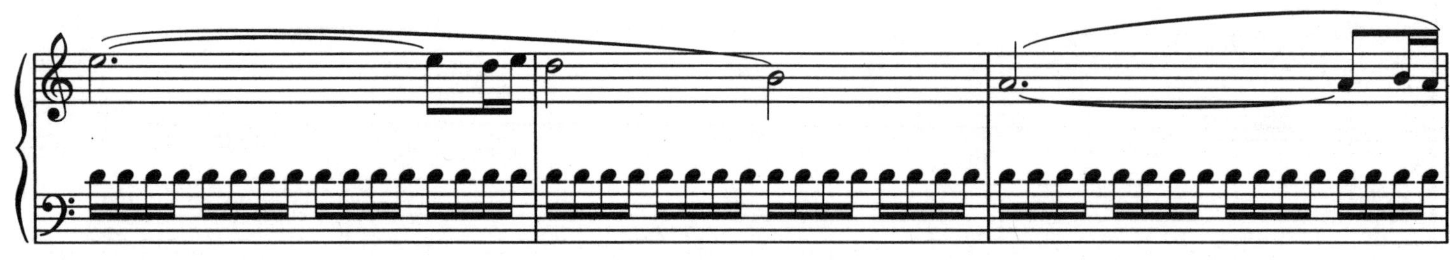

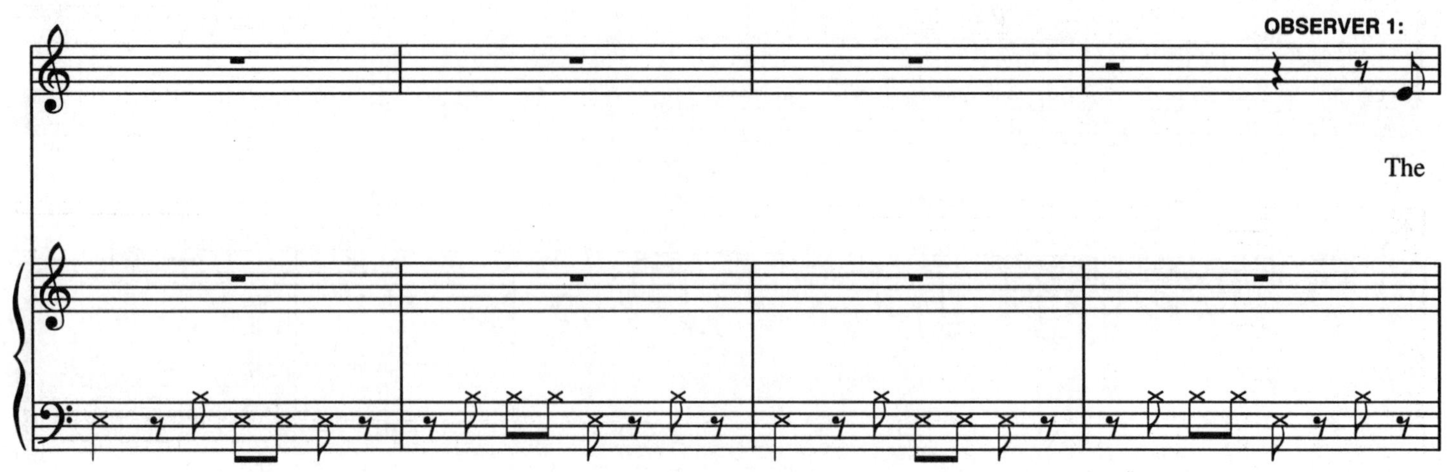

© 1975 & 1977 by RILTING MUSIC, INC.
All Rights Administered by WB MUSIC CORP.
All Rights Reserved International Copyright Secured

OBSERVER 2:
eye sees, the thought flies. The eye tells, the thought de-nies. I will pre -
pare for your re-turn - ing. (Is there no oth-er way?)
(Bell plate) (unmeasured accel.)
mp
pp
sempre pp
sempre p
(steady tempo)
dim.
sempre p

OBSERVER 1:
The
OBSERVER 2:
word falls, the heart cries. The heart knows the word's dis-guise I shall ex -
gliss.
gliss.
pect you then at eve - ning. (Is there no oth-er way?)
gliss.
OBSERVER 1:
The
(Drums continute)

bird sings, the wind sighs, The
air stirs, the bird shies. A
OBSERVER 2:
storm ap - proach - es.
(There must be oth - er ways.)
OBSERVER 1:
The leaf shakes, the wings

rise. The song stops, the bird
flies.
The storm ap -
OBSERVER 2:
proach - es. I will have sup - per wait - ing.
(Hand drum)

OBSERVER 1:
The song stops, the bird flies. The mind stirs, the
heart re - plies: "There is no oth-er way, there is no oth-er way."
OBSERVER 2:
I will pre-pare for your re - turn, I shall ex-pect you then at eve-ning.
(bell plate)
(unmeasured accel.)
pp
(steady tempo)

mp
pp
sempre
dim.
OBSERVER 1:
The word stops, the heart dies. The
gliss.
wind counts the lost good-byes. There is no oth-er way. There is no
gliss.
gliss.
oth-er way.

(Bell plate)
(unmeasured accel.)
dim. poco a poco

Cut from the Musical "Company"

Multitudes Of Amys

Music and Lyrics by
Stephen Sondheim

Molto rubato (♩ = 120)

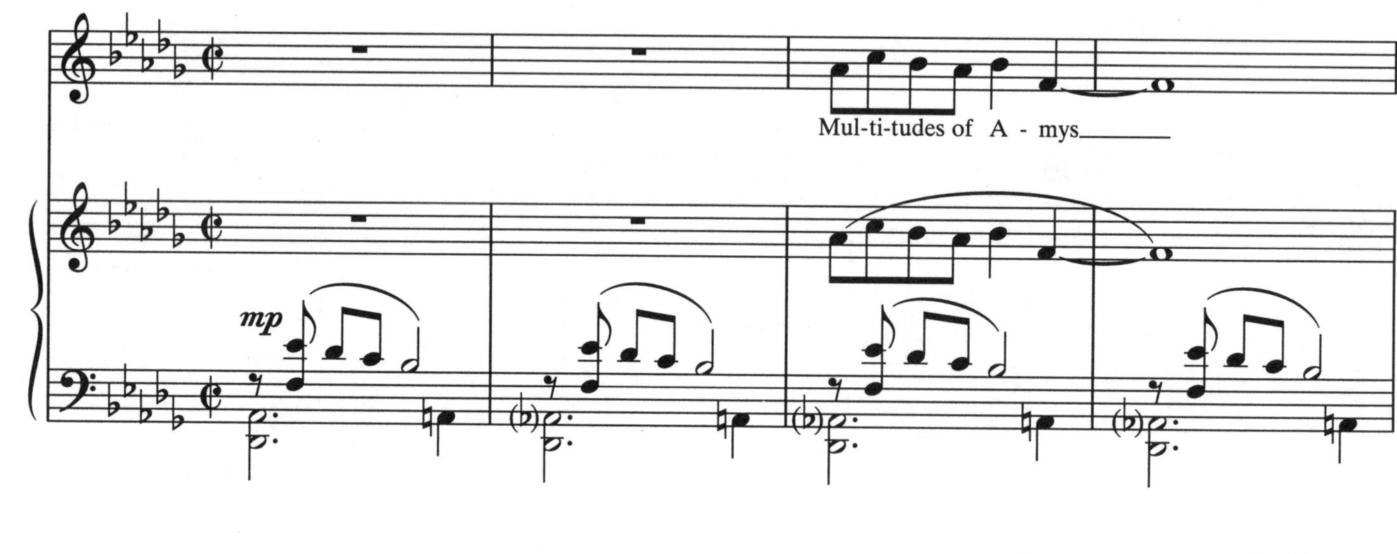

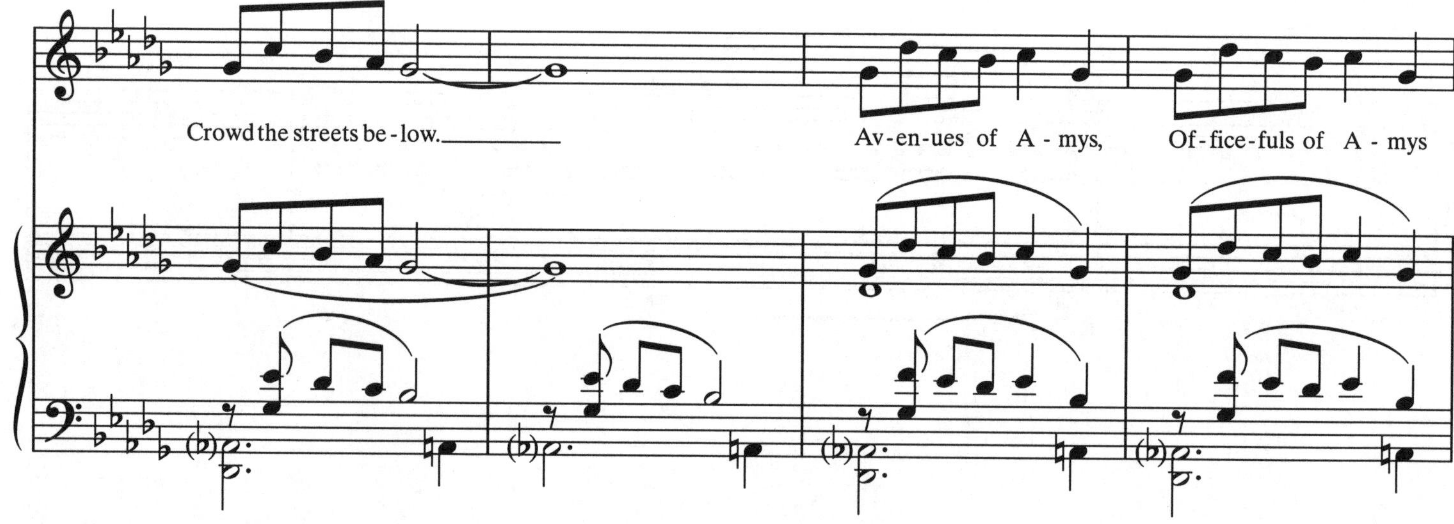

© 1991 RILTING MUSIC, INC.
All Rights Administered by WB MUSIC CORP.
International Copyright Secured All Rights Reserved

con molto
won-der what it means.
I see them wait-ing for the lights, Run-ning
for the bus, Mill-ing in the stores And hail-ing cabs And dis-ap-
poco cresc.
rall.
a tempo
pear-ing through re-volv-ing doors. Mul-ti-tudes of A-mys,
rall.
a tempo
Ev-'ry-where I look.
Sen-ten-ces of A-mys, Par-a-graphs of A-mys,

Fill-ing ev-'ry book.
Won-der if it means
I've gone to
rall.
piec - es.
Ev-'ry oth-er word
I speak is
some-thing
she says.
poco cresc.
cresc.
rall.
a tempo
Walls hang with pic-tures of A-mys,
Gal-ax-ies of A-mys
dot the night skies,
a tempo
mf
Girls pass and look at me with A-my's eyes.
poco dim.

I've seen an au-di-ence of A - mys Watch a cast of A - mys act in a play.
Seems there are more of her ev - 'ry day.
What can it mean? What can it mean?
rall.
I've caught a
rall. cresc.
a tempo
sta-di-um of A - mys Stand-ing up to cheer,
a tempo
mf

Chor-us-es of A-mys, Sym-pho-nies of A-mys Ring-ing in my ear.
I know what it means, Hey, A-my, I know what it means. Oh, wow!
accel.
rall.
I'm read-y, I'm read-y, I'm read-y
accel.
cresc.
rall.
a tempo
now!
a tempo
f

All that it takes is two, A - my, Me, A - my, You, A - my.
cresc.
f

poco dim.
I know what it means, Hey, A - my, I know what it means. Oh, wow!
mf
f
I'm read - y, I'm read - y, I'll say it:
cresc.
molto rall.
Mar - ry me now!
ff
molto rall.
3

From the Musical "Sunday In The Park With George"

Move On

Music and Lyrics by
Stephen Sondheim

© 1984 RILTING MUSIC, INC. (ASCAP)
All Rights Administered by WB MUSIC CORP.
All Rights Reserved

you've gone.
Just
keep mov - ing on.
I
chose, and my world was shak - en - -
so
what?
The
choice may have been mis - tak - en,

the choos - ing was not.
You
have to move on.
poco dim.
p poco rubato
Look at what you want, not at where you are,
p
poco rubato
not at what you'll be.
Look at all the things you've done for me:

non rubato
op - ened up my eyes,
evenly
taught me how to see,
no - tice ev - 'ry tree,
un - der - stand the
light,
con - cen - trate on now.

I want to ex-plore the light. I
want to find how to get through, through to some-thing
cresc. poco a poco
new, some-thing of my own- -
cresc. poco a poco
move

on.
Move
on.
Stop
wor - ry - ing if your vi - sion
is new.
Let

others make that decision -- they usually do.
You keep moving on.
mp
Piu mosso
Look at what you've done, then at what you want, not at where you are, what you'll be.
allargando
Look at all the
dim.
mp
allargando

things you gave to me. Let me give to you some-thing in re - turn.
poco rall.
a tempo
See what's in my eyes
And the
poco rall.
mp a tempo
col - or of my hair
And the way it catch - es light
cantabile, tenderly
And the

care
cresc.
And the feel - ing
f
And the life
sub. f
mov - ing

on.
We've al - ways be - longed
to - geth - er!
We will al - ways be - long
to -

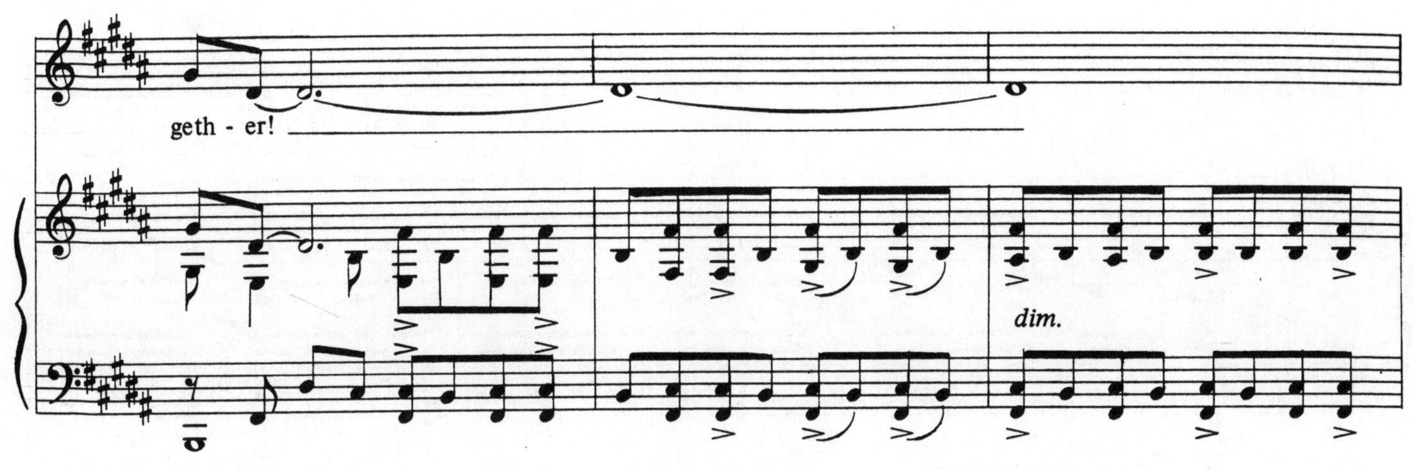
geth - er!
dim.

Just keep mov- ing on.
dim. poco a poco

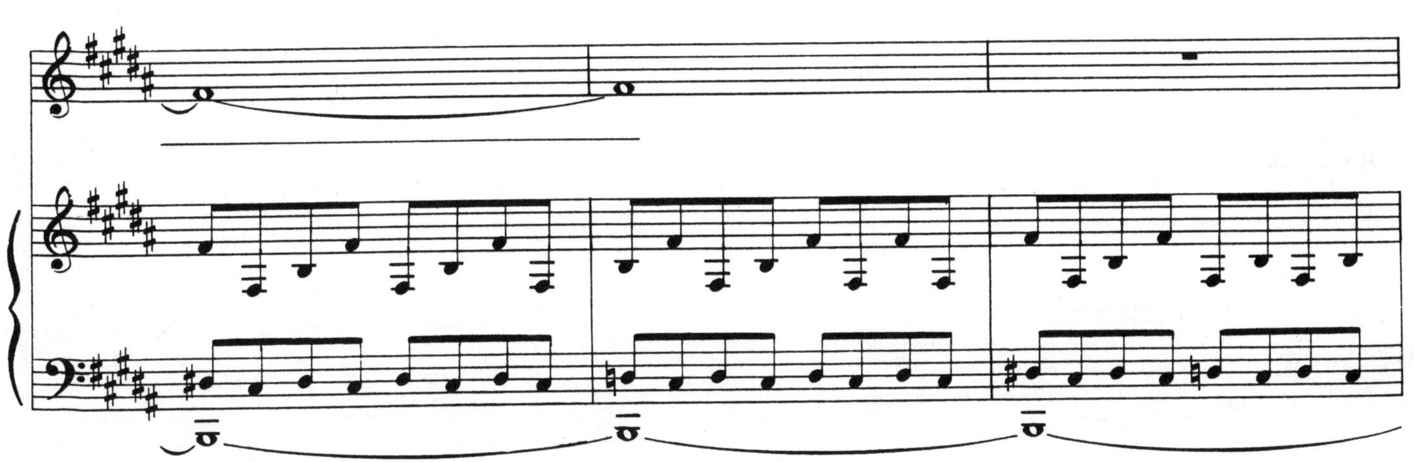

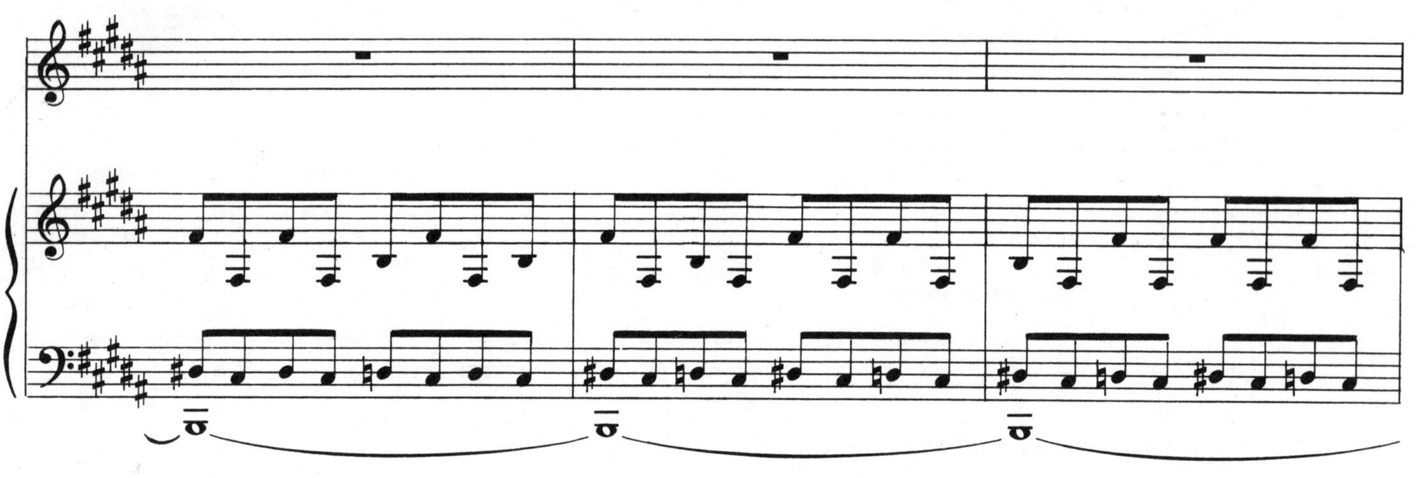

p Meno mosso
An - y - thing you do, let it come from you. Then it will be new.
p

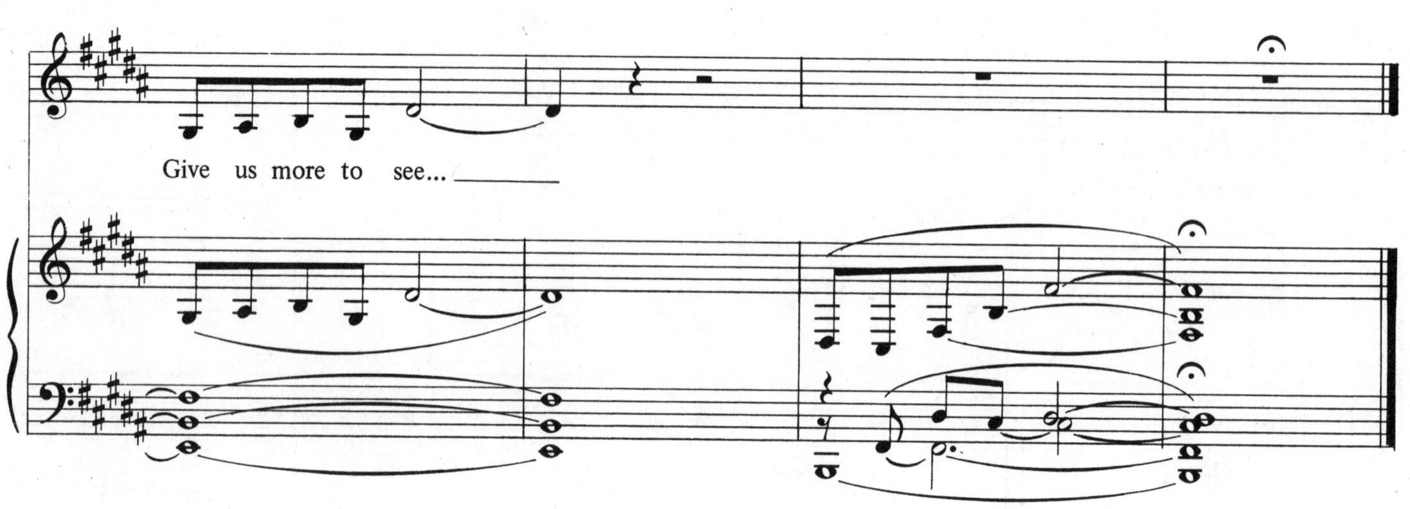
Give us more to see...